Don't Let The Rocks Cry Out

VOLUME III

PASTOR DON R. VINING

ISBN 978-1-969865-40-4 (Paperback)
ISBN 978-1-969865-41-1 (Ebook)

Inquiries and Book Orders should be addressed to:
Leavitt Peak Press
17901 Pioneer Blvd Ste L #298,
Artesia, California 90701
Phone #: 2092191548

This book is dedicated to my loving
parents, Kie and Geneva Vining,
from whom I draw much strength and wisdom.
Mom has always been that praying giant in the faith
that has caused great victories to come to many lives.
Dad, on the other hand, has had only
one cure for every aliment in life---
"WORK, and things will get better." While I exercise
the lessons learned, I have found that a praying
heart and hard working hands can accomplish
mighty things for the Kingdom of God.
With heartfelt gratitude thanks, Mom and Dad.

Contents

Acknowledgments..ix

Foreword..xi

Introduction xiii

1. **From Laziness To Pentecost** 1
    Unique; Not Weird 2
    Rejoicing in the Past..3
    Be Prepared 5
    What is Pentecost?...6
    The River of God 9
    The Guilty Silence 11
    No Praise Too Excessive 14

2. **The Difficulty of Silence**.............................. 18
    A Vile Silence 20
    Where's the Power? 22
    Rock and Roll...24
    God's Perfect Timing...25

3. **The Example of True Praise** 32
    From the Inside Out 33
    What is True Praise?...36
    Distant Distractions...37
    Reaching Higher 39
    Exultant Worship 41
    Social Worship 42
    To Each a Gift..43

4.   Perceiving vs Knowing.....................................49
     New Arenas..51
     Truth Flows Out...53
     Biblical Boasting.......................................53
     Spiritual Sadness Seeks Seclusion.......................56
     Hidden Treasures..59

5.   Giving Back...61
     Is God in the House?....................................62
     Back to the Basics......................................64
     Soul Concentration......................................66
     Excellent Examples......................................69

6.   God's Praise Concert......................................72
     Is He or Isn't He?......................................77
     The Pentecost Insignia..................................80
     Determined Seeking......................................84

7.   Head or Heart Knowledge?..................................85
     Bury the Tail...91
     Worthy of Valleys.......................................94

8.   Reasonable Praying..97
     A Close-In God...101
     The Soul's Duty..102
     Paul's Exhortation.....................................105

9.   The Confidence Level.....................................108
     Wake Up the Soul.......................................110
     Go Ahead, God..114
     The Happiest Condition.................................116

10. Praise in Action...118
     Spiritual Flashbacks...................................120
     What is True Praise?...................................121
     The Evidence of True Faith.............................127

11. Genuine Worship.. **129**
   Who are You Living For?.....................................131
   Rejoice in Tribulation 133
   The Work of Suffering.......................................135
   The Offering of Praise.......................................138

12. Confidence **141**
   The Rock of Our Salvation...............................142
   Moving Forward..145
   Particular Ministries...147
   Christ's Lineage...148
   Enthusiastic Praise..148

Acknowledgments

I thank my beautiful bride for her strength and much Godly wisdom for standing by my side. Thanks also to my two daughters-Sheena, who is Beautiful inside and out and Brittany, who is like a Lion so proud of these two. Thank You, Lord, for these blessings.

My thanks to Connie Neumann for another job well done in taking hundreds of pages of notes, and capturing the message that I believe will bring divine healing to thousands of lives.

My gratitude to Dr. Carol Bartholomew for an out-standing cover design that flows with the subject of this project.

Foreword

There is no limit, no end, and no measure to the goodness, grace and mercy of God! If there are no boundaries to God's goodness, then why do we set boundaries on our praise to Him? Pastor Don R. Vining has tapped into the answer to your every need, your every question------**PRAISE**. Pastor Vining has a true gift from God to take the most profound knowledge of God's Word for our lives and spell out its meaning with such great simplicity. If you want to know God's will for you, praise Him! As this book so readily shows us, God inhabits the praises of His People! Inhabits! That means "meets you where you are!"

Don't Let the Rocks Cry Out is yet the most liberating book in Pastor Vining's first three books of his series. He begins with the foundation of Christ for our lives with *Salvation, It's Not What I Thought It Was*. And then is the must read *Souls Under Siege*, a compelling encouragement for the trials we face as we search for our "place" in Christ. Now the answer to our fears and questions is in *Don't Let the Rocks Cry Out*. My life has been forever changed by this author's passion for God.

As I anxiously await a new revelation from the pen of Reverend Don R. Vining, you can know there will not be a rock crying out in my place. God is my peace, my strength, my comfort, my wisdom. My salvation! My

hope! My provision! Has God done anything good in your life? Then *DON'T LET THE ROCKS CRY OUT!*
-Suzi Scott,

Director of Early Childhood Education

Introduction

The term "Pentecostal worship" is often misunderstood. In this book, I will use it to describe a style of worship, rather than a particular denomination. Pentecostal worship, as used here, is high-energy worship, worship with lifted hands, or a way to give praise to the Lord with a loud voice. The term is not meant to offend or criticize the beliefs of others.

Regardless of your denominational background, my goal is not to get you to change churches. The goal of this book is to suggest that there may be more than one way to worship the Lord. Our God is a big, awesome, mighty, powerful God who loves to hear and see the praises of His children. The Scriptures say, "The Lord inhabits the praises of His people" (Psalm 22:3).

If you are Pentecostal, I challenge you to seek a higher place in your worship. If Pentecostal worship is new to you, look closely at the Scriptures and see what God has for you.

I pray this book will draw each of us into freer, more intimate worship of the King of Kings and Lord of Lords.

CHAPTER ONE

FROM LAZINESS TO PENTECOST

Pentecostal worship is different from any other type of worship in the world. It is supposed to be different. It is a unique experience. When a stranger or a bystander sees Pentecostal worship, it's supposed to compel them in. A Catholic friend of ours came to one of our services and was speechless. The more he thought about it, the more unique things he picked out about our style of worship-- the music, people standing, people raising their hands, people clapping, people bowing before the Lord. He said it so intrigued him that he just had to check it out again. So much went on that he couldn't even grasp everything that was coming at him.

Before he came, he was skeptical, so 1 challenged him to come to one service a month to let us minister to his spirit. I promised him that he would have a changed life forever and that he would see things about this God he has chosen to serve that he had never seen before. In fact, I promised him that he would be a Pentecostal by the end of the twelfth service.

UNIQUE; NOT WEIRD

I believe that when Pentecostals worship the way God designed them to worship, it's going to intrigue and compel people to come in. Pentecostal worship is not strange, weird, or of the devil. It is unique.

Many Pentecostals attempt to water down their worship so they don't offend. We want to bring people in, so we lighten the load of what we really believe as far as worship is concerned. "Well, we clap every now and then, and sometimes somebody will stand and raise their hands." "Do y'all shout?" "Well, occasionally. Every once in a great while, somebody shouts." We've watered down Pentecostal worship so much that we're often not any different from anyone e

We should be compelling people to come and worship like we worship instead of other folks coming in and compelling us to be like them. My Catholic friend said, "Man, I'm telling you, the Spirit of God is in this place. I am a changed person here."

When we worship in such a way that our hearts begin to minister to other hearts, people's lives are going to change. No longer can we tell people, "You can't wear that, and you can't do this, and you can't sit there, and you can't go over there, and you have to give this much, and you gotta do that." We can't live like that if we're going to win a lost and dying world. In true worship, we are not judges. It is not our business what the person sitting next to us is all about. We have a responsibility to love them and not be inhibited in our worship.

Early in my ministry, friends would come who had never seen me as a minister, and I would water down and get totally nerved out about what I was supposed to be in the pulpit. I thank God that He delivered me from that. I know when I go with my heart, someone's life is going to be touched, changed, delivered, and set free.

Someone asked me if I get nervous before I sing. I said, "No, I'm either going to do good or bad. I've settled that. But I'm never going to get better unless I practice." I'm never going to worship like a Pentecostal should worship unless I practice worship. If I want God to move in a Pentecostal way in my life, if I want the gifts of the Spirit to operate in my life, then I have to know how to worship Him.

REJOICING IN THE PAST

Look at what Luke says in chapter 19, beginning with verse 36:

And as he went, they spread their clothes in the way. And when he was come nigh even now at the descent of the mount of Olives, the whole multitude of the disciples began to rejoice and praise God with a loud voice for all the mighty works that they had seen.

Notice they weren't worshipping and praising Him for what He was doing, but for what He had done. This tells me that if I never see God do another thing, I need to be praising Him. I need to be giving Him honor and I need to do it with a loud enough voice so somebody can hear me. People may say I'm a nut, but praise God, there's something alive inside me. I think we need a few more radicals. I didn't say fanatics, and 1 didn't say a bunch of nuts, but I think it's time for us to get radical in our worship.

If you're going to pray correctly, you start by worshipping the Lord. You thank Him and praise Him and honor Him for all the mighty works He has done. Luke 19:38-40 says,

> Blessed be the King that cometh in the name of the Lord: peace in heaven, and glory and in the highest. And some of the Pharisees from among the multitude said unto him, Master, rebuke thy disciples. And he answered and said unto them, I tell you that if these should hold their peace, the stones would immediately cry out.

It's intriguing to think a rock or a stone could praise God in my place. I began to do a little research, and prayed, "Lord, what exactly are You saying here?" He had some amazing things to say to me.

If you have ever felt the power of the Holy Spirit working in your life, you're a wonderful candidate to become a Pentecostal worshipper. Being Pentecostal simply means that you flow in the Spirit. If the Spirit tells me to get up and worship, I'm going to get up and worship. If the Spirit tells me to run, I'm going to run. If the Spirit tells me to weep, I'm going to weep. If the Spirit tells me to get up and shout with a loud voice, I'm going to get up and shout with a loud voice. That's what Pentecostal worship is all about.

1 have a real burden and a real passion to break our lazy way of worship. It's time for us to let someone know that Jesus Christ is alive. He saved me, delivered me from sin, took my life out of bondage, raised me up out of the valley, and healed me of a disease the doctors said would take my life. He has done so much in my life, that if I can't do anything else, I should be able to make noise for Him.

In this passage, Jesus said to the Pharisees, "You know what, I can tell them to hush up, but they would absolutely burst, and the rocks would cry out before they could keep in what is inside them."

That's why Jeremiah said, "It's like a fire" (Jeremiah 20:9). I don't know if you have ever been burned, but I have. It doesn't take me long to get my fingers off the stove.

When the Spirit of the Lord is working in and through and around your life, you can look back and think about where God has brought you from. I'm not talking about the fact that whatever's going on in your life today hasn't worked out yet. Look back at what did work out. Did you know that all of the things of the past worked to get you to this place in your life? God does all things in His time.

BE PREPARED

A while back, someone gave me a really comforting word. I had said to this person, "There are enough finances out there to do what we feel God wants us to do at our church, but they seem to be blocked out and locked up like a dam. If that dam were ever set free, this ministry probably wouldn't have financial dilemmas. I want to pray, believing that God will unstop the dam." This person, looked me square in the eyes and said, "If it was all released right now, this day, you wouldn't know what to do with it. Look at all the leadership training that needs to happen. look at all the different areas of ministry God is bringing into place. You're not ready for it, Pastor. If you were, you would already have it." I thought a lot about that. Right now we're training and discipling leaders, and beginning to pull some things together that will be a lasting work.

WHAT IS PENTECOST?

What does it really mean to be "full of the Spirit"? Am I full of the Spirit if I still live like I've always lived? Is getting saved all there is to it? When you begin to worship God in a Pentecostal way--with some energy and some action---it is because God has delivered you and set you free from your bondage. He's brought you out. God didn't leave us in the miry clay. He brought us out and set our feet on the Rock. He made a place of security for us and said He was the cornerstone of our lives. He is everything we need to live a righteous and holy life. He has given us everything we need in the Bible. All we have to do is read it.

Some people have no idea where the Pentecostal movement started. They think it might have started down at the Handy Way. Actually, it started in the book of Acts. My Bible tells me the Lord Jesus Christ challenged about 540 people and said, "Here's what I want you to do. I've trained and discipled you, but there's one thing still lacking. You need to be empowered and indued with the Holy Spirit. You need Pentecost to be set alive in your life."

He told them to go to the upper room and to shut their mouths. He told them to open their spiritual ears and to get in one mind and in one accord. He said to quit being the judges of mankind, and become a vessel the Spirit of God can flow through. Out of those 540, only 120 showed up. The 300-plus who didn't show up were probably at the Handy Way.

But the Bible says on the day of Pentecost, when they were all in one mind and one accord, the Holy Spirit was poured out like a mighty rushing wind, like the fire of God. They didn't know where it came from; all they knew was the Holy Spirit showed up. They were so changed when the Holy Spirit fell upon them that they began to speak in other languages. At that particular time, there were hundreds of thousands of people from the entire world in the city. What a time for the Holy Spirit to fall! What a time for the Holy Spirit to show up and do a work!

He's going to show up just when we don't think He will, and He's going to start touching the hearts of Catholics, Mormons, Presbyterians, Methodists, Pentecostals, Assemblies of God, and Churches of God, and on and on and on. At Pentecost, business men on the streets were saying, "Wait a minute, that guy's speaking my language, and he doesn't know my language."

Years ago, at a revival in a church in Ocala, Florida, the meetings were led by an evangelist who was just this little short guy, but a real live wire. While he was there, he had a Spanish lady start ministering to a young Spanish girl. He would say, "The Lord loves you," and the lady would translate for the young girl. Before you knew it, he was speaking in some other language. He looked at the girl and tears were streaming down her face. He looked at the interpreter and asked, "Do you understand what I'm saying?" "Yes sir," the lady replied. "You're speaking in Spanish." God changed the man of God's language into Spanish so he could reach the one who needed to be reached.

I have a really serious problem with those who call themselves Pentecostals, but show no evidence of a real life change. We keep doing the things we've always done. We say we serve a Pentecostal God, and we're full of the Holy Ghost, but then an old friend shows up and finds out we're the same old person we were forty years ago. If we're going to serve God in the way He wants to be served, and if we're going to touch people's lives in the way He wants lives to be touched, we have to understand that if we don't praise Him, the rocks are going to cry out in our place--- and that is not God's desire. Jesus said He could tell the disciples to hush, but if He did, the rocks would cry out.

It's time for us to get ourselves in a place where the upper room experience can come. When those followers left the upper room, they were changed. Their voices had changed, and the language they spoke had changed. I don't mean from English to Spanish, but I mean the way they spoke and the things they said, and the words that came out of their mouth. There was no doubt a change had taken place in their life. Instead of walking around, saying, "Oh me," they walked around as people with a destiny.

THE RIVER OF GOD

The river of God flowed right out of the upper room. You have heard about Ezekiel's dream, the vision, where the Visionary stepped in ankle-deep water. He went on down the creek a bit, and it was knee deep. Then it was waist deep, then it was chest deep, then it was neck deep, and then it was so deep he had no choice but to get in it and go with God (Ezekiel 47:1-5). If you research the place where Jesus was crucified, the Bible says water and blood flowed out of His body. The same distance the dream talks about--- from the time the water was nothing until it was way over your head, gushing out of the house of God--- is the same distance the Bible talks about from where Jesus was crucified to the upper room. The flesh, the water and blood that flowed out of the body of Christ flowed into the ground, and true Pentecost started at the cross. It was first ankle deep, then knee deep, then waist deep, then chest deep, then shoulder deep, until it was over their heads. That's why the Bible says the water flowed out of the threshold of the house of God. That was the upper room. Where did it flow from there? What happened to the 120 who were there? They began to disperse all around the world.

We have a reason to get together and worship. We have a purpose because God gave His only Son on the cross at Calvary so His blood and His anointing would flow to the upper room. The upper room was so full of God's power and anointing even the house of God couldn't contain it all. It began to gush out and flow to all the ends of this earth. Jesus Christ gave His life, rose from the dead, and ascended into heaven. Then He got out of the way and let the Holy Spirit do the work that needed to be done. And the Holy Spirit came in power.

We have to allow this Pentecostal thing to get into our spirits. I'm tired of being like I've always been. God is moving. God is pouring out His love and His Spirit.

Our finances are not the problem. The problem is in preparing ourselves. We have to get the sin out of our lives so that when we show up at church, God Himself is already moving in our midst. That's true Pentecost.

Do you know what caused the commotion in the upper room? They began to shout and praise God. They didn't stick their heads out the window and say, "Let me see if my brother is out there. I don't want him to see me acting like this." No, they got totally lost in the Spirit. They said no rock would cry out in their place. They said, "I'm going to make noise. I'm going to go with my heart and with my spirit. I'm going to get on my feet, clap my hands, and dance before the Lord, thanking Him for what He's already done. They not only thanked Him for all His mighty acts, but by faith, they praised Him for what He was *about* to do.

We have to learn to respond to what God is doing. Have you ever felt the Lord speak to you during a service, telling you to stand and raise your hands, but you have continued to just sit there? Has He spoken into your heart and said, "Just say 'amen'," but you wouldn't do it? You might as well have slapped God in the face. He's working on our behalf, He saved us out of a life of sin, He's given us hope, peace and joy, and all He asks is that we worship Him.

THE GUILTY SILENCE

Let me share a few comments different writers have made about this passage in Luke 19. In *The Biblical Illustrator,* J. Parker, D.D. called this Scripture,

> *Guilty Silence in Christ, because our Savior means to intimate that this silence would be vile. Let us then proceed with this dismal business and arraign this fearful silence. We tax it first with the most culpable ignorance that one could ever have.*

This is talking about the times we have something to praise God about, but we keep silent. You may not like some of what I'm going to say--- my big toes are sore, too, after reading this passage. God has an opinion about how we worship. When I really take a good look at this, I know God doesn't do things the way I think they should be done.

At our church, I'm the one who makes sure the bills get paid. I thank God for the way our folks give, but sometimes, when we get it all together, it just isn't enough. It's easy for me to whine, "But God, You promised," instead of saying, "Lord, if You never give me another miracle, I thank You for what You've already done". Our church has already done more than the entire community said could be done. We've already accomplished more in our lives and in our faith than we ever dreamed possible.

I sometimes think God doesn't break out in a rally of miracles because we don't recognize them when they do happen. We take them as though they are a quarter in our pocket; no big deal, just another miracle. But the Bible says we should praise God for what He's done and for all His mighty works. It was a mighty act of God to save me from a life of sin. We have something to praise God about.

> *If you found a man who was entirely insensible to Milton's Paradise Lost, or Coopers Task, dead to the touches of Raffael's pencil, to all the beautiful, sublime scenery of nature, to all that is illustrious and inspiring in human disposition and action, you would be ready to say, "Why, this senselessness is enough to make a stone speak" (J. Parker, D.D., The Biblical Illustrator).*

When we look around and see all the beauty and all the creation of God, we should break forth in praise for the Creator.

We went to the mountains recently, and just stood in awe. It is something to behold, to think Almighty God could just speak, "Let there be mountains," and poof--- they showed up. If people can see all the beauty and scenery of creation and all God has done in their midst--- even before they asked Him to--- and not be moved to praise Him, it would be enough to make a rock speak! That's what Jesus is saying. If He were standing here today, He would say "Hey guys, listen, I know they're making a lot of noise, and I know they may be a little too energetic for you. I know you may not like that chorus, and the color of the carpet may not be just right, and the music may be too loud, or too fast, or too slow, and the preacher may be a little crazy, but if I told these disciples to shut their mouths, the rocks would cry out." The disciples were so full of the mighty acts of God and had seen so much of Christ's anointing---so many miracles, so many saved from a life of sin, so many set free, so many demons cast out--- that our Lord said He couldn't shut them up if He wanted to, because if He did, the rocks would cry out in their place.

Sometimes, we get on a spiritual high, talking about how God touched us and set us free, but all someone has to do is walk up and say, "Boo!" and we get scared and run back. Then God has to do His first works all over again. That's what Scripture talks about. It is a shame that I know people whose lives are full of sin, but who give the Almighty more praise for the creation than believers do. I see people in restaurants drinking their beer and smoking their cigarettes, or with a reputation for beating their family members, but they'll take a moment to bow their heads and pray over what God has blessed them with that day. I can look over my shoulder and see people, who spend their lives serving God, who won't take three seconds in public to say, "Father, I'm not ashamed."

We should get excited about what God has already brought us through. He has already told us we don't have to worry about what we're going to wear, what we're going to eat, or where we're going to work. We don't have to worry about how much money we're going to have, what kind of family we're going to get, or what kind of automobile we're going to drive. He said He's already taken care of all those things. He is so far out ahead of us that we couldn't catch up if we tried. His glory has paved the way for a lifetime for us. All He wants is for us to remember all of His mighty acts, and every day, He wants us to worship Him.

Lately I've been praying, "Lord, I've never been a really good worshipper, but I'm about to get better at it." There have been times He told me to say, "Hallelujah, Amen, and praise the Lord," and a million and one times I've held back. But I'm not going to hold back anymore. There have been times I felt Him calling me to stand up and dance before Him, but I didn't do it because I was afraid of how someone might look at me. I don't care any longer what people think of my style of worship. I'm going to go with God and I'm going to worship Him. No rock out in that field is going to have cause to speak on my behalf.

NO PRAISE TOO EXCESSIVE

> *Men may be undeserving of the praise they obtain; or if the praise be deserved in the reality, it may be excessive in degree; but there can be no excess here. It is impossible to ascribe titles too magnificent, attributes too exalted,*

adorations too intense, to Him who is 'fairer than the children of men,' who is the 'chief among ten thousand, and the altogether lovely. Now to be insensible to such Being as this, argues, not merely a want of intellectual, but of moral taste, and evinces, not only ignorance, but depravity. He who died not for a country, but for the world and for a world of enemies---He awakens no emotion, no respect. Shame, shame! (J. Parker, D. D., The Biblical Illustrator).

Sometimes we desire praise we shouldn't be concerned with, and at other times, we go a little overboard giving praise to individuals. There isn't any way, however, that you can give too much praise to the Almighty. And when you hold back one little tidbit, when you hold back one little praise report, then a rock has every right to speak in your place.

We are depressed, oppressed, in a dilemma; we're frustrated, hurt, and don't know which way to turn. We're up today, and down tomorrow. We have faith tonight, but there's none to be found in the morning. It's because we get so wrapped up in right now, and in what may---or may not---happen tomorrow, that we lose the advantage of living in the abundance of right now. Fear of tomorrow and anxiety over the past keep all but a very few truly living in abundance. Christ offers us not only life, but abundant life (John 10:10).

What is "right now"? For me, right now is thanking God the bills are paid up through today. Right now, I can thank God I had two or three meals today. I don't know what is going to happen in the morning, but I know about right now.

The only way your family heritage can die is if you stop living it. The only way the Pentecostal heritage can die in our lives and in our communities is if Pentecostals stop living what they proclaim to be. Through the course of time, many have come by and said exactly what they said to Jesus: "Tell them to shut up and hold their peace. Tell them it won't work."

Too many have whispered that God doesn't move the way He did forty years ago, and though with our heads we said it wasn't true, part of it seeped into our hearts. Those of you who are new to Pentecostal worship haven't seen true Pentecostal worship yet. You haven't seen an alcoholic walk in drunk as a skunk, fall at the altar, stand up and go out as sober as sober can be, because people were worshipping and praising and honoring the Almighty. Pentecostal worship is not coming to church shouting the walls down, and then going out and doing the same things you did before. That is not Pentecost.

When Scripture talks about the rocks crying out, it is saying that when we act so ignorant about what God has already done, it is enough to make a rock speak. I want to challenge you to put aside your lazy style of worship and walk into every church service ready for Pentecost to happen.

I have found that people are hungry to know more about the Holy Spirit and Pentecostal worship. J. Parker said, "We charge this silence, secondly, with the blackest ingratitude. I need not enlarge on this hateful vice.

The proverb says, 'Call a man ungrateful, and you call him everything that is bad." We're so busy wanting more things to happen, we're not giving praise for all the mighty acts He's already brought. We'll pray, "Lord, give me more, give me more, give me more." How about praising Him for what He's already done? How about thanking Him that you made it this far? When you feel like sleeping in on Sunday morning, go ahead and get up anyway, because if you don't show up, a rock just might cry out in your place. It is time to take the commitment we made to the Lord and get radical about what the King of Kings and Lord of Lords has done in our lives. It is time we grow up in the Lord and let the true Spirit walk before us.

I challenge you to repent before the Lord for allowing rocks to take your place. Ask the Lord to enliven your spirit and remind you of the things He has done in your life. Ask Him for the freedom to raise your hands or lift your voice in praise.

God is doing something in the midst of His people and I don't want to miss it. Tell the Lord you love Him, and tell Him you're sorry for being a lazy worshipper. Tell Him that when He lays it on your heart give him praise, you're going to. Then stick to the promise.

CHAPTER TWO

THE DIFFICULTY OF SILENCE

I'm tired of walking alone. I'm tired of trying to figure it all out. I want the Lord to surround me. I want my step to be His step and my words to be His Words. It doesn't matter what I went through yesterday. It doesn't matter what I've gone through in the last thirty-eight years. It doesn't matter what I'm about to face tomorrow. I want to know how to better praise Him.

Today, you may need to pray, "Lord, my life is swamped and covered with sin. Surround me and take the sin away, and replace it with truth and righteousness." He saved us. He was our hope when we didn't deserve hope. He was our passion when there was no passion. If we don't praise Him, the rocks are going to cry out. No rock is going to speak on my behalf.

I am not interested in being the same person I have always been. I am not interested in always wanting more, more, more, more, more, and more.

Look again at the passage in Luke 19:37. It says, "the disciples began to rejoice and praise God with a loud voice for all the mighty works that they had seen." They didn't praise Him for what was coming. They didn't praise

Him for that particular moment, but they praised Him for all they had seen. They praised Him for everything that had already taken place. I believe with all my heart that some of us miss what God has set and predestined for us because we're so wrapped up in tomorrow---when we don't even have a promise for tomorrow. He never said we'd wake up in the morning. All we really have is a guarantee that we are going to stand here right now.

The Bible says the disciples worshipped with all that was within them; they worshipped for all the mighty works they had already seen Him do. They say

> *Blessed be the King that cometh in the name of the Lord: peace in heaven and glory in the highest. And some of the Pharisees from among the multitude said unto him, Master, rebuke thy disciples. And he answered and said unto them, I tell you that if these should hold their peace, the stones would immediately cry out.*

I began to think about that Scripture, and I said, "Now Lord, I just cannot picture a rock speaking." God said He would use the foolish things to confound the wise, and to me, it just doesn't get any more foolish than to think a rock is going to cry out if I don't. Yet, the Bible tells us if we don't cry out, the rocks will. They will speak on behalf of what the Master has done. It's crazy to think the Lord would have to resort to getting praise from a rock. I began to research this and asked, "Does a rock literally speak?" I asked the Lord what He meant, and asked Him to help me understand.

What I learned is this: I'm ready for the Lord to get the glory He deserves. If I think back to where He has brought me from, I could praise Him for the next forty years. He saved me, sanctified me, and filled me with the Holy Ghost. He healed me of leukemia and of a nervous condition. And when the entire community said there couldn't be a church in Summerfield, God created a church in Summerfield. We have so much for which to give Him praise.

A VILE SILENCE

I asked the Lord what this verse meant, about the rocks crying out if I didn't. According to J. Parker, the Savior means this silence would be vile. We need to talk about this silence, for it is a fearful silence. I hope the Lord won't let you sleep tonight until you give Him the praise due His holy name. I hope the Lord will let you feel like there's a mountain resting on your chest---until you give Him praise. When the Lord spoke this, He was saying some things, we need to understand. He was try-ing to say, from the bottom of His heart, how awful it is for you to keep your peace and not speak out about what God has done.

In this passage, the Lord is really telling the Pharisees they'd have to be ignorant to tell the disciples to shut their mouths about what they had already seen. They had seen Jesus raise the dead, save the lost, heal the sick. They had seen Him make brokenness into holiness, seen Him bring peace and take people from the valley of the shadow of death and raise them up. The disciples had seen Jesus take those who were persecuting others and make believers of them. "So, Pharisees," Jesus said, "you have to be nuts to think they're going to hold their peace. If I tell them to shut their mouths they will, but it would be as dumb to ask them to do that, as it is to think that a rock could speak." He was really saying that if He wanted to tell them to hush, they couldn't. There was too much in them, it was like a fire. They'd seen too much, been through too much, to turn back on Him.

I don't understand how some of us can serve the Lord for many years and then turn our backs on Christ. I don't under-stand how anybody can walk into the midst of a Spirit-filled place and think, *I'll sure be glad when the preacher gets finished.* I don't understand that, because if you hold your peace, and I hold my peace, Jesus said the rocks are going to cry out in our place. No rock is going to take my place. He said it is the vilest ignorance you can ever begin to comprehend for them to keep their peace. He was saying, if you disregard all of nature and take things that are of great value and that have become a cornerstone for your life, and pretend you don't see them, you are dumb as a rock.

How is it we can make a covenant with God in our time of need, and then when all is well, turn our backs on Him? How is it these crazy Pharisees could say to the Lord, "We know what they've seen and what they've gone through and what they're all about, but we still want you to tell them to hush." The Scripture tells us, in Galatians 5:16, that if we walk in the spirit, we will not fulfill the lust of the flesh. That tells me they were of a fleshly mind. Some of us are like them: we can't figure out what God is doing. You may as well stop trying to figure it out. I have. Every time I say I'm not going to do something, the Lord says, "Yes, you will." And just about every time I say I'm going to do something, the Lord says, "Hold on."

When you're full of the glory and you have experienced salvation, and when you've seen God take you out of the valley and bring life and breath into you and those around you, you can't keep your mouth shut. Jesus was saying that He knew the future of the disciples. He knew they were going to be in the upper room. He knew Pentecost was going to be poured out on them. So he was saying to the Pharisees, "Boys, if you think it's hard to keep them quiet now, wait until they are indued with power." When you've had an experience with God, the world shouldn't be able to shut you up. You should be so powerful in your approach that the world has to shut its mouth and listen to what you have to say.

WHERE'S THE POWER?

Some of us say we are Spirit-filled, but there is no power in our walk because we're halfway in the Spirit and halfway in the flesh. We say Jesus can deliver everyone else, but He can't deliver us. God wants a people of purity, of holiness. He wants a people who come together and say, "Father, 1 don't care how much it hurts, I don't care what I have to give up, I don't care what I have to sacrifice, I'm ready. No rock is going to cry out in my place. No rock is going to steal my joy." Jesus said it has to be the vilest ignorance one can begin to comprehend to hold your peace. To see all of His beauty and creation and then sit there and shrug as if it means noth-ing... Well, the way we say it where I'm from, "You ought to be slapped." If it weren't for lawsuits, I would give all of you permission to give a holy slap.

Get up on your feet and praise the Almighty. Didn't He save you? Isn't there faith in you? Get up from where you're sitting and go tell someone. Some of you will say, "I believe you, but I ain't a-going to go out there." You can't give too much glory. Take this Scripture to heart and say, "Lord, there are a lot of things I praise." I praise my family all the time.

I'm proud of them. I brag about our church every-where I go. If I can do that for my family, then I can get up and raise my voice and say, "Yes, God's been good to me, but let me tell you what He's done for my soul. He went straight to hell, and He took the keys to death's hell." Did you know the devil doesn't even have keys to his own house? And yet some of you fear him. Jesus went and said, "Lucifer, give me those keys." The devil doesn't even have the keys to his own house, but some of you have given him the keys to yours.

If you go home and say, "I'm going to praise and honor Jesus. Lord, let Your blood come one more time and cover my life," then the devil can't stay. You'll hear a little jingle, and it will be your keys flopping up against the wall. The devil will say, "I'm out of here. I can't take it. I can't take that noise; I can't take it when they bring up the blood. I can't take it when they bow down and worship Him. I have to get out of here."

The more you praise God, the more He shows up. Some of you sit in church thinking, "I want to get up, but I've been so bound to keep my dignity, I hav- en't done it." Why don't you do something you've never done before? Why don't you raise your hand and make a shout to the Lord this day? Tell the devil, "Ain't no rock going to cry out in my place." Jesus will fill you with the Holy Ghost right in the midst of your worship. You don't need a preacher to touch you; all you need is a spirit of worship. To keep silent is the most ungrateful thing you could ever do in your life. We're like spoiled-rotten babies, saying, "*Give me*, Lord. Give me salvation, give me peace, give me money. Let my boat come in." You sit there when you have an opportunity to worship, and it is the most ungrateful thing you could ever do.

We need to quit coming to the Lord asking what He can do for us. Instead, we need to ask, "Lord, what can I do for You? You've done enough for me. If You never give me another job; if You never bless me again; if I die with cancer in my body, I will give You praise for what You've already done." Jesus said if they kept their peace after all they'd already seen, the rocks would cry out. For those of you who like it quiet, I am so-o-o sorry. Being quiet isn't me. I'm probably going to get up on Monday morning and open my window and say, "HEY, ROCK, you ain't going to speak in my place today. I've got praise in my heart. I have a song in my spirit. Jesus is going to speak through my life. HEY!"

ROCK AND ROLL

If you want the deaf to hear, the blind to see, and the lame to walk, get into worship. Shut those rocks up.

Get on your feet and say, "Jesus, I praise You for what I've already seen You do." Some people don't like the term "rock and roll" in the church, but I'd rather roll into heaven, than slide into hell any day of the week. I'm going to rock for Jesus. I'm tired of my life sliding away. I'm tired of trying to be some dignified somebody. That isn't working anyway. I'm glad for what Jesus has done in my heart. I can't wait to go tell someone in the restaurant, "Look what Jesus did."

"The ungrateful," says Locke, "are like the sea; continually receiving the refreshing showers of heaven, and turning them all into salt." South says, "The ungrateful are like the grave; always receiving, and never returning." But nothing can equal your ingratitude if you are silent (*The Biblical Illustrator*). If we have ourselves received the knowledge of Christ, we are bound to impart it. We get too wrapped up in what we want, instead of getting wrapped up in what is right.

GOD'S PERFECT TIMING

I like vehicles, and I especially like new vehicles. Recently, I worked out a deal on a $40,000 truck. Man, you talk about sharp. Diesel engine, CD player, it had the works. I felt okay about my reason to have it. I felt okay about the cost, I felt okay about the payment. I felt okay as far as my family was concerned. It would serve us better for things we enjoy doing. The Lord said He would give us the desire of our heart, so I went to the bank and filled out the paperwork. I called the car lot and was supposed to go on down there Friday, but I didn't. I was supposed to go Saturday, but didn't. I was supposed to go Monday, didn't, supposed to go Tuesday, didn't. Finally, on Wednesday, I went to the bank. I felt great about the truck, but something in my heart was different. After I signed the papers, I went home and took a little nap before the service. In my dream, I woke up and that truck was right there. I said, "Lord, what meaneth this? I feel okay about this thing. It isn't a selfish thing with me." You see, when your worship is a selfish worship, you get nothing out of it, and God is not going to protect you in your selfishness. From that moment on, unbeknownst to my family, I got on the phone and tried to get hold of the bank. *I don't want it, I don't want it, I don't want it.* I couldn't get hold of them until I was at the dealership the next morning, ready to turn in my old truck. The banker asked what the problem was and I said, "How are you going to feel if I tell you I don't want this thing?" She said, "We understand. We know you by now, so we'll just rip the papers up." I began to tell her all the reasons I wanted the truck and all the reasons I felt maybe it wasn't good timing. She said, "Both are right and I don't think you're wrong by going with the truck. After that, I really had another peace about it. So I said, "Thank you. I'm going to go sign the papers at the dealership now and I'm going to drive my new truck." When I got there, I sat for two hours, waiting on them to bring my paperwork. A preacher friend was there with me, and he said, "Man, what's up with you? You look troubled." I said, "You know, I have some of the most wonderful people on the face of the earth at our church in Summerfield. I've been asking them to sacrifice, to buy property, to start a preschool, to do this and do that. And they've been willing. They're giving and going beyond. But I'm troubled about this." He looked at me and said, "You are a man of God, and you're doing just fine. Go for it". Another man came in to sign paperwork, and I found out he was a preacher, too. Three preachers in the same room. We talked about everything but the truck, but while we were talking, about every seven or eight minutes, I came up with something else for the salespeople to give me and add to the deal. The salesman finally said it was going to be a while. I told him I needed to leave, but I said,

"Give me something to drive, and I'll come back in a while and sign the papers." Now you know, in the business world, you don't add a bunch of changes to a $40,000 deal and then say, "Praise God, on my word, I'll sign the papers when I get back." But they loaned me a rental and told me I could sign the papers later. My pastor friend and I stopped for a bite---that's a sandwich for those who don't know--- and before we were finished, my cell phone rang. It was the dealership, telling me they had a problem with this and a problem with that part of the contract. I said, "We don't have a problem, you have a problem. We're already under contract. I don't care if you have to burn that truck, you are going to stand by your contract. The man beat around the bush, and finally said they needed to take some of the extras off. I said, "Sir, get the key to my old truck; I'll be back in five minutes." That surprised him, because he thought I was already back in Ocala. Do you know God will sometimes put you on hold around the corner to work out some stuff for you? Before I could drive five minutes back, the manager of the dealership called, but I didn't take the call. I told my friend, "They've already worked it out. They don't want any more money and they don't want me to cancel out the deal." I walked back into the dealership and the boss met me right at the door. He told me what they'd worked out, but I said, "I'm not interested in what you have to say. For ten days I've been troubled deep down in my spirit. I knew in my head it was okay, but when you argued with me over $350, it was like God saying, 'Son, I know it feels right to you, but the timing is not good timing." The man looked at me and said, "You are a man of God and you done got yourself a confirmation." He gave me a high-five and handed me the keys to my old truck. I've never been so happy.

Coming back on the interstate, I called my wife and she asked if I got the truck. I said, "You won't believe it. 1 backed out." She sighed, relieved, and then said, "I have been an absolute nervous wreck, but I didn't want to disappoint you because I want you to have it. I felt like all the reasons were right, but the timing was off". It was the heat of the summer, and during the summer, church giving goes way down. We rob Peter to pay Paul, but someday Paul's going to get more than Peter has and we won't have to rob him anymore. That's where my faith is. She said, "I've been troubled about this thing." Before I got back to the house, she had made out my track payment and said she'd never been so proud to put a payment in the mail in all her life. I tell you all this for a reason. Even when you think you're right, and your motive is pure with the Lord, sometimes He stops us when the timing isn't right. And that's something to praise Him for. We must be a people who don't let the rocks cry out. We've gone too far to stop now.

If you haven't had anything recently to praise Him for, think about when He saved you. Some years ago, a lady in our church fussed and fussed---day and night---about the trailer she and her family were living in. "Oh, that trailer we live in..." Gripe gripe, gripe. I thought, "Dear God, deliver her. Do something with her." During a storm one night, a tree fell on the trailer. She came in crying, "Oh! My house!" I said, "Hold it. You griped about that thing, but now the insurance said they'd pay it off, get you another one, give you piece of land to put it on and get you out of that rental park. And you're going to gripe about it? You'd better not let the rocks cry out, sister." God does things like that for us, but we're like a horse with blinders on. Take the blinders off. Look around and see His beauty, see His holiness. We were blessed to drive through the Cherokee mountains a while back, and it seemed that every mile there was a place you could pull off and see the scenery. I thought we would never get there. My ears popped more than popcorn and I said I felt like a popcorn machine. We finally got to the top of the mountain and I'll tell you, it was breathtaking. All I could say was, "My God, My God, My God, My God." All He had to say was, "let there be mountains," and there were---and there are. He said, "Lot there be salvation," and there is. He said to the Pharisees, "I could tell my disciples to hush, but it won't do any good.

They've already seen too much." We've already seen too much, too; we can't back out.

We have to press on, keep moving, because the rocks are going to cry out if we don't. You say you don't feel like praising; you're too sleepy. Wipe the sleep out of your eyes. Listen, God has a desire for you to prosper. He doesn't have any problem with me driving a new ride. The truck was not the problem. It was the timing. God will work it out for you. He has some stuff for some of you just around the corner, but the only way you're going to get there is to praise Him. You're going to have to shut those rocks up. The more you hush those rocks, the more you're going to hear His voice.

God is a good God. Not long ago I said, "Lord, we need a financial miracle. People are giving to the church, but we can't keep going two and three thousand dollars in the red". Two days later, somebody walked into my office and laid 1,000 dollars on my desk: "This is to help the church." I said, "Thank you, Jesus." That person may never understand how much that will help and how much they were in the will of the Lord. We chose not to buy the new truck. My publisher has been sending me little old piddly checks every month for book sales. I thought, you couldn't pay off a cockroach with a suitcase like this. Then one day they sent me a check for $841, for books that had been sold. God sold those books way back when, because He knew there was going to come a time for me to choose between what I wanted and what was best for me. When you sacrifice before the Lord, it doesn't go unnoticed. He knows where you are. He knows what you need. He just wants you to praise Him.

He wants you to say, "Lord, I'm not worried about more, but I'm going to praise You for what You've already given me. I'm going to praise my way."

Jesus loves you, and He wants you to acknowledge that He is God. As long as you give your heart to Him and serve Him as best you can, He will make a way, for He is the way. Right now, as best you know how, stop where you are, lift your voice and praise Him.

CHAPTER THREE

THE EXAMPLE OF TRUE PRAISE

I believe that when we get in the Word and begin to understand the importance of worship, it has to enliven something. I wake up spiritually not---just expecting the Lord to save, heal, or bless us financially---that time is now. We must get intimately involved with worship. Jesus plainly said that if we don't praise Him, the rocks are going to cry out. I believe studying worship is going to help us respond to our families and our problems better, so we can do more than just say, "Well, I think I'm in the light."

As I was praying with a young man one Sunday evening, I asked him what he wanted. He said, "I don't know if I'm saved. I don't know what it feels like or what it looks like." When I asked him if he knew what sin was, he said he wasn't sure, so I explained it to him. You know, it took just three minutes to help him understand what sin is and how we're all born into a life of sin. I told him if he'd pray a simple prayer with me, believing it with all of his heart, and if he'd cry out to Almighty God---like screaming at a football game---God would do something on the inside. I told him that when he left, he wouldn't have to go home wondering. He could go home knowing. I took the young man by the hands and began to pray with him. It seemed like every other word his grip tightened. "God, I'm sick of this life, and I'm sick of this style. I'm tired of the worrying; I'm tired of the fear; and I'm tired of not knowing." You could see God begin to move in his life. I can guarantee you don't have to ask him if he is saved. You can see the difference; you know something is going on.

FROM THE INSIDE OUT

The same thing happens when we understand true worship from the inner man. Something is going to come alive in you, on you, and around you. No matter where you go, people are going to know you are one of the peculiar people the Word talks about. I used to say I just wanted to be normal, but I've decided that living a Christian life is just about as abnormal as it gets---as far as the world is concerned. It isn't normal to go out and praise God when you wreck your car. It isn't normal, when you get bad news in the mail, to praise God any- how. It isn't normal to smash your finger half off your body and say, "Hallelujah! It will probably fall off, but the Lord will grow another one." There's really something about serving the Lord in the way we worship. We praise no matter what comes our way.

I'm a Pentecostal because I enjoy the movement, I enjoy the feeling, and I enjoy seeing what it does in people's lives. I don't think there's any worship like Pentecostal worship. I don't think there's any enjoyment quite like Pentecostal enjoyment, because I not only pray my friends through to the Lord, but I can raise my hands and worship at the same time. The Pentecostal movement teaches me about being filled with the baptism of the Spirit---meaning when I don't know what to say or how to say it, the Spirit will take control and begin to pray for me and through me. I love when I go out and speak a word, and then go home and scratch my head, thinking, *wow, where did that come from?* Don't you enjoy that? That's a part of being Pentecostal. That is a part of saying, "Lord, let the Holy Spirit embed this Word in my heart and let it be fused to my spirit. I don't want to just hear it and forget it. I want to hear it and remember it." You can talk about a Scripture and learn something from it, and two or three months later, you can come back to the same Scripture and find something you never knew before. It's because you can never understand the fullness. His Word is so great.

Worship is so incredible that every time we reach a certain level, the Lord says, "Hallelujah! I'm pleased. This is good, but watch this. I have another level for you." I'm tired of this level. This level is great and wonderful, and is changing a lot of lives. But I'm ready to go to another level, just like you can't go to the fourth grade until you conquer the third grade. There comes a time when we have to say, "Lord, I've known this all my life, but surely I've missed something along the way."

When people ask you to define your style of worship, tell them it's unique. It's different, it's fun, it's exciting, and lives are being changed. If you want to experience something unique, come with me.

A Baptist boy who was very educated in the Baptist movement came to our church and laughed at me for many, many weeks because of our style of worship. One Sunday evening, he said, "Preacher, I have fought you all night long." I didn't criticize his beliefs; I just made sure we understood we were serving the same God. I wrapped my arms around him, and he began to weep like a baby. The next week, he came and brought another Baptist friend, who simply said, "I think I'm saved, but I'm not sure. I really don't know." And the Lord opened the door.

In Psalm 34:1-3, David writes:

I will bless the LORD at all times: his praise shall continually be in my mouth. My soul shall make her boast in the LORD: the humble shall hear thereof, and be glad.. O magnify the LORD with me, and let us exalt his name together.

He wrote this after he had changed his behavior and had experienced a change in his life. Every time you experience a spiritual change, the Lord gives you a freshness, a fresh word. Every time David went through a valley---or even a high time---the Lord gave him something to make a story or song or praise report out of. Sometimes, he made a plea out of it. Did you know that when you're in the valley, it's okay to plead? "Oh God, how long shall I stay in this valley? Lord, surely You are there, but I don't see You anywhere. I don't feel You, and I haven't heard from You in a long time."

The purest thing you can do in worship is to share your heart. I believe there is too much two-faced

Christianity. We say we believe one thing, but we hide other things. If there's a problem in your life, you shouldn't hide it. You should con fess it and say, "I'm having a problem here. I'm saying and doing things I shouldn't." Even if you don't have peace to say it to someone else--- and sometimes that's better--- at least get in your prayer chamber and say, "Father, You said You'd be a friend who sticks closer than a brother. I need to talk to You. I'm struggling in this area. Lord, I want to worship You with the fullest worship, but I can't because there's something holding on." True worship will help you let go and let God do what He wants to do. Look at verse one: "I will bless the Lord at all times: His praise shall continually be in my mouth." He didn't say His praise would be there every now and then, or when everything was going well. He didn't say His praise would be there when he felt like it; he said His praise shall continually be in my mouth. In other words, the psalmist, is saying there has to be an act of true praise.

WHAT IS TRUE PRAISE?

True praise is thorough and to the fullest. There is no true praise without the concentration of the soul. You can praise in your head all you want. I can tell my wife I love her, but it won't mean a thing until my actions begin to say from my soul, "I love you." Then it begins to attach to her soul and she understands what I'm talking about. How many times have we spent days and weeks and months worshipping, but it wasn't thorough? It wasn't the kind of praise where the soul was speaking to the soul of God. It was the kind of praise where, in my mind, I was worried, fearful, and full of pain. Sometimes we think, *I'm going to praise God now that I'm in pain, and maybe He'll take the pain away.* David is saying it isn't that kind of praise. How do I know? Because he said that His praise would continually he in his mouth--- in the good times and bad times, an the rich times and poor times, in the happy titles and sad times.That means when the church is doing well, and when it isn't; and when the doctor says there isn't anything else he can do for you.

Generally, God will come through and perform a miracle after we've done everything and gone every place we can. Because then, when He performs a miracle in your life, your neighbor can't say, "Well, the doctor did that." Sometimes, we have to go through these things so that there will be true, unadulterated, praise. Praise to the utmost.

DISTANT DISTRACTIONS

Distracting forces are widespread and abundant. It's easy to go to church and say, "Lord, I'm praising You," while we're worrying that we don't have money for the car payment. "Lord I'm remembering You, but I don't know how I'm going to make it through this week." There are many distractions keeping the soul and heart from tuning in to what is really going on in the home. How many has spent year, after year, after year, after year in relationships or with your children, and when you really take a good strong look at who you're living with, you find out they're a bunch of strangers? It's because your soul has never really clicked in. Have you ever attended a particular ministry for a year, three years, seven years, twelve, fifteen, or twenty years... and still feel like a total stranger in your own church? Could it be because you've been so settled on singing those same three choruses and saying, "This is my seat"? I know people who will leave a church if you sit in their seat. You know, every time I find one like that, I go sit in his or her seat. We should be versatile. We should understand that God loves us so much. He brought us to this place. But He loves us too much to leave us here. He wants us to continually grow.

That's why people who have worshipped the same way for forty years are coming and saying, "I don't know what's going on, but don't be surprised if you see something out of me." I want to see something. I want to see people get freed in worship. I want to see people get the freedom to raise their hands and praise Almighty God. I want people to see that this idea of needing a preacher in order to be saved is *junk*. You don't need a preacher. You just need faith in the faith you have, and to say, "Lord, it's me and You; that's all I've got. Lord, I'm out here in the middle of nowhere and there isn't anyone to worship with me, but I'm going to give You 'soul' worship. I'm going to worship You, Lord, until You're sick of me worshipping you. You're going to get so tired of me calling on You that You're going to move me to another level."

I know a couple of little girls who, when we say "no" to them, if it's something they really believe in, they will press through. I know a little girl (not one of mine) who got a new dress for a particular youth camp meeting. Every day she wanted to put that dress on, and her mama would say, "No, no, no. It's for your special party at youth camp; you can't wear it now." When she was dropped off at youth camp, Mama hadn't gotten back in the car before the girl came out with her brand new dress on. There wasn't anything Mama could do about it. That girl believed in wearing that dress, and her mother finally had to say, "I don't care if you wear it every day, you're at youth camp and that's all that matters to me."

REACHING HIGHER

If you really believe in true worship, you're not going to be satisfied with what you've always had. You can't take the Pentecostal experience you've already gained and experienced thus far in your life and just sit there and say, "Well, that's all there is." You know what happens when the apple stops growing. In just a few days, a good ol' wind is going to come up, and ---poof!---it's gone. The very day you sit there and say, "This is it; this is as far as I'm going," be prepared to dry up and fall off the vine.

A person doesn't grow if they don't mean to grow. If you make up your mind you're not going any deeper in this thing, no problem. You don't hurt anyone but yourself. But I'm saying, "God, for a long time, I've worshipped You in my head and now I'm ready to worship You from my heart." This praise David is talking about is constant praise, in every department of action. Intellectual, artistic, commercial, political---in every area, every office, division, and aspect of your life, there is constant worship. When I'm sitting on the side of the road getting a hundred---dollar ticket, deep down, there's still a love for God. And when the doctor says, "You spent all your money, but there isn't anything I can do for you," there's still something bigger going on in my heart. Even when my toes are being chewed on, there's still a constant prayer. There's still something in here that happened way back then that's like a burning fire. It won't go out. It's like a bed of coals. You can cook over a flame and make a decent meal.

I called my dad over to a camping place out in the forest a couple of years back and said, "I'm going to cook; don't bring a thing." I had some aluminum pans, hamburger meat, potatoes, carrots, butter, onions, you name it, it was in there. I wrapped it all up, and he asked what I was going to do with it. I said, "Stand back, Pop, and watch." I dug the coals out and stuck the pans under that fire, and Pop said, "Boy, I can smell the Handy Way com- ing." But about 40 or 45 minutes later, we took those pans out, uncovered them, and he said, "We ought to do this more often." I'm telling you, it was good stuff. Listen, it's okay, when the flame's burning. It's okay to come into a place when God is moving in an incredible way. But do you know what's better than that? When true worship, constant worship, is going on in your life. It's a never-ending worship. You'll be worshipping at midnight.

Some days, I get home and all we talk about is how tired we are, how exhausted from all the hard work and the long hours but---then the phone rings, and somebody says, "Look what God is doing, look what God is doing." That's wonderful, but often I want to say, "You don't have to dwell on what happened three or four days ago. You don't have to keep living off what happened to you twenty years ago." We're talking about a constant worship.

David was saying that every moment of every day there was constant worship in his soul. In every circumstance of life---joy, sorrow adversity, prosperity, bereavement, friendship---and in every area of your life, there should be this kind of worship. The Psalmist says, "I will bless the Lord at all times: His praise shall continually be in my mouth." When I'm being chased by the devil, there is still praise. Many of us have the idea that when the devil comes after us and starts messing with our heads, we're whipped, defeated. We forget about that constant flame. The Bible says that the gifts and the calling of God are without repentance (Romans 11:29). He has planted His faith seed in you. Every devil in hell can chase you, but you're victorious as long as you'll praise the King and as long as you'll keep moving ahead. Even when you have a down day, when you weren't a real good testimony, or a week, a month, or even a year in your life when things weren't the way they should be, it's okay. Just understand there's an ongoing flame, deep down.

EXULTANT WORSHIP

God is the sum of total worship, or total of all excellence. He is the One of all joy. Have you ever felt joy? Take that joy and multiply it by several billion times and that is the joy of Almighty God. That is the joy we are capable of tapping into by simply worshipping Him.

Worship---because He is the fountain, because it is His joy. It is okay to boast in Him. The Bible talks about boasting on the negative side. We shouldn't boast about ourselves, but when it comes to boasting about the Lord, if we don't, the Bible says the rocks are going to cry out. It says if we don't get involved with total worship---letting the total soul worship and honor constantly---that is grounds for the rock to cry out.

SOCIAL WORSHIP

Here, I think, is what separates Pentecostals and non-Pentecostals. A true Pentecostal---a true worshipper---becomes magnetic, drawing others to the shrine before which he falls. A true worshipper draws people. Have you been in awe as you watched someone who was totally lost in the presence of the Lord and in worshipping Him? A person like that is like a magnet.

When the Bible says you are the light of the world, it's actually saying you are magnetic. When you go out into the world, people see something they've never seen in an individual before, and they want what you have. They see you smiling when you should be frowning. They see you energetic when the doctor said you just have a few days left. When you're broke as a skunk, but still living like you're wealthy, you become magnetic. People, want what you have. A sweet lady who had been searching for a church home visited our church and sent word she'd found her home right here---said she'd found a place to roost, if you will, because she felt the worship of Almighty God in this house. She wanted to find a place where people would worship with their hearts, where they wouldn't judge, criticize, and spend more time looking at each other than at God. I tell our people, if they're coming to church because of me, they're going to be let down. I guarantee it. I'll probably pass them on the highway and put them in the ditch without meaning to, or something else will happen. I encourage them to get their eyes off me. I'm not perfect. I'm worshipping the same God they're worshipping. I'm seeking a higher level of worship just like I'm trying to encourage them to do. I'm keeping myself on the straight and narrow just like we should all be doing. God called me to help lead our congregation and be an inspiration to them. God called me so my life would be magnetic and would draw people to Him. I would rather people be drawn to me and my relationship with Christ, than have them be drawn to me for what I could offer them.

TO EACH A GIFT

Every person has a gift or a talent, and it is important that you use it. Some can use a shovel; some can use a paintbrush. Some can push the sweeper and some can mow the lawn. Some can clean the john, some can flip on the lights, and some can receive the offering. Some can sing, some can preach, and some can work with the babies in the nursery. (I thank God I don't have to go in there. I don't mind feeding the babies. It's what happens after feeding the babies that is more than I can handle.) But whatever your gift or talent, it is important to use it. God intends to take your talent and make you magnetic in His service and in your worship, so that it will draw other people to Him. If it's your gift to dig ditches, God's going to call other ditch diggers by your actions. But there is real danger when you have gifts and talents and stop using them for the Lord. You must use your talent.

What is the reason for true praise? Psalm 34:4 says, "I sought the Lord, and he heard me, and delivered me from all my fears." He didn't just hear me, but He delivered me from every fear I have. That's why the Bible says, "fear not, fear not, fear not, fear not," 365 times. All through the Word, He shows He is the one who delivers mankind from fear and anxiety. David's reason for true praise was that he had been delivered out of all his troubles. His troubles were great in their variety and number, but he was delivered. By the testimony of David, I am confident I can worship God because of what He has already delivered me from and what He's about to deliver me to. He's always taking you out of something, to lead you into something else. He didn't tell the Israelites, "Hold on, I'm going to deliver you to the hate land," He said they were going to the Promised Land, the land of milk and hone.,

Why should we get out of head worship and into heart worship? Because of what He has done for us, our past deliverance. Think back to where He brought you from. Things change when the soul man is hooked up with the God man, when the Holy Spirit speaks to our spirits, and when hearts speak to other hearts. When you speak from the head, you go home and think, *I shouldn't have said that.* But when you get into a predicament, the Spirit within you automatically speaks up and says, "That's okay.

That's what grace and mercy are all about." David was delivered out of all his troubles by prayer. Some of you want God to deliver you, but you haven't prayed about it. Some of you just sit there whistling, waiting for your boat to come in. David said, "I sought the Lord."

I remember there was a boy at school whose mouth I had had enough of, so I sought him out. I didn't stop until I found him. I didn't wait for him to come to me; I went to him. And when I got there, he knew this was a person he had never seen before. He had seen the body before, but he had never seen the intensity, and probably had never experienced a bloody nose like he did that day. Sometimes you need to ball your fist up in the devil's face and tell him you've had enough of him, and you're going to blacken his eye and bloody his nose. Don't let the enemy lead you on a wild goose chase. Sometimes we have to wise up and say, "This isn't soul knowledge---this is an attack against my mind."

I heard a little story about a blonde gal who went out to her mailbox, looked inside, slammed it shut, and went back into her house. About ten minutes later, she came out again, walked to the mailbox, looked inside, slammed it shut, and went back into the house. About the seventh or eighth time she did that, the neighbor came out and asked her what in the world she was doing. She said, "I've had enough. My computer keeps telling me I've got mail."

I spoke at a church that had two Sunday morning ser vices. During the first service, I only had a certain amount of time, so I preached like a wild man. The second service was a little more relaxed, because I had a little more time. I don't know what happened, but all this funny stuff started coming out of my mouth. I guess the people needed to laugh, because God still moved. "A merry heart doeth good like a medicine: but a broken spirit drieth the bones" (Proverbs 17:22). Before you take another pill, take time to laugh. If you say there isn't anything to laugh at, go look in the mirror. That will crack you up.

Make a resolution to bless and thank the Lord. Here are some things for which we ought to bless and thank the Lord: temporal, spiritual, personal, family, national, and Christian. There are plenty of things for which to worship the Lord. If you had a roof over your head last night, you have a reason to praise Him. He's blessed you with life, with a way to go, with friends and family, and with clothes to wear. Even if you don't have all those things, everybody is blessed in some way. Like David, praise Him for what He's already done. In Luke, Jesus was saying that the disciples were praising Him for all the mighty works they'd already seen. He wants us to worship Him.

When you pull up in the driveway and hit that little button so the garage door comes up, praise Him. When the rose bush that doesn't have one leaf on it strikes a bloom, and a flower comes out, praise the Lord. There's always something to praise Him for. When you have to mow the yard, praise God there's a lawnmower to mow it with. God wants us to bless Him with every aspect of our lives. You complain that you went fishing and didn't catch a thing. Thank God you had the time to go fishing. David is saying, "Praise Him constantly. I'm going to praise Him even when I don't feel good, even when I'm on the backside of the pasture and all my brothers are about to be chosen as king. I'm still going to praise the Almighty: I still have something to worship Him for. We are to bless the Lord, the giver of all. There is no mercy except for that He gives freely, boundlessly, always---even when we don't deserve it. And my friends, we don't deserve the blessings.

A resolution to bless the Lord is one of which even nature approves. "All thy works shall praise thee, O LORD; and thy saints shall bless thee" (Psalm 145:10). According to *The Biblical Illustrator,* it is a resolution that reason sustains and which Scripture models and encourages. It is a resolution which is an analogy of the customs of social life and which works in accord with our obligations. A resolution that harmonizes with the employment of the heavenly inhabitants. A resolution which, if carried out, will contribute much to life's happiness and promote the glory of God and all of our actions in life.

"I will bless the LORD at all times: his praise shall continually be in my mouth" (Psalm 34:1). Why? For all the past things He has done. Everything is worth praising God for---even when you get mail that doesn't make sense, or phone calls you don't like. Even when things aren't the way they should be, think about where He's brought you from. Think about what He's done in your life. Think about His grace and His mercy. We have something to be happy about. We are a blessed people. We're saved, sanctified, and He's filled us with the power of His Spirit. He speaks to us. David said he would constantly praise the Lord---every step of the way, every day, through every valley and every mountain.

God loves you and He deserves to be praised. If you hold your peace after all you already know, it would be just as dumb as expecting a rock to cry out. Please don't let the rock cry out on your behalf. Don't govern your praise by what you feel right now. God's working a process in you. Instead, look where the process has brought you. Look what He's already done…. and give Him praise.

CHAPTER FOUR

PERCEIVING VS KNOWING

A s I continue to search my heart about worshipping, serving and honoring the Lord, I have come to the conclusion that worship is the answer to what so many are battling and struggling with. We can give counsel, advice, money, and do all we know to do, but when it gets right down to it, it will depend on our true worship of the Lord. We're talking about Pentecostal worship--- worship that is supposed to be lively, something that breathes life into the lives of others.

Never in my life have I seen so many families being battled against, and so many differences within the home as I'm seeing lately. And it isn't about one little issue; it's major issues, things that need to be dealt with. Somehow, we have to get out of what we *perceive* to be God and get into what we *know* to be God. I had to get out of what I perceived salvation to be, because it's different. The Word says, "Restore unto me the joy of thy salvation; and uphold me with thy free spirit" (Psalm 51:12). I can guarantee the joy of His salvation is different than the joy of my salvation. We can dance, shout, hoot and holler with the best, but the real issue is the truth of the matter. There comes a time when it is either God, or it isn't. He either heals, or He doesn't. He either brings strength---

and is your strength---or He isn't. He either truly spoke to you, or you were mistaken. The Bible says that as you draw unto the Lord, He will draw unto you (James 4:8). As I tap into this arena of praise and true worship,

He's going to touch me. That's what the Word says: "Bring ye all the tithes into the storehouse, that there may be meat in mine house, and prove me now herewith, saith the Lord of hosts, if I will not open you the windows of heaven, and pour you out a blessing, that there shall not be room enough to receive it" (Malachi 3:10). Too many are trying to prove the Lord and it isn't working. It could be because of what we have perceived to be truth and righteousness and holiness.

I'm ready to stand on the truth and be a true Pentecostal worshipper. There are too many watching the way we worship, too many lives at stake. When someone comes up to you in the grocery store, crying their eyes out because of a crisis they're going through at that time, it is either real or it isn't. God wants to change lives, but we have to be sure we're not just cheerleaders. We must divinely believe that God is a sovereign God. We either believe He is the healer, the deliverer, or we don't. If you get on a backhoe, you expect the backhoe to dig a hole like a backhoe is supposed to; you're not expecting a backhoe to act like a box blade. You can't buy a cat from the cat store and expect it to bark like a dog. Neither can you come in and act like you're from some other part of the moon and say you're a Pentecostal worshipper.

You either know it's God or you don't. And if you don't know, but you want to, then seek God about it and be sure what you perceive is the true God. Because, my friend, Christians ought not be confused. My Bible tells me that fear and confusion do not come from the Lord (see I Corinthians 14:33). If they don't come from the Lord, where do they come from? I've learned to read people. If what they are doing in the name of the Lord confuses me, if their style of worship confuses me, then I have to believe it can't be of God, because if it were of God, my spirit would bear witness. In other words, I would know for sure. There isn't anything worse than going to church and seeing God move and then going home and wondering if that was God. We need to know.

NEW ARENAS

I don't think you have to belong to the Church of God to go to heaven. I think you have to know Jesus Christ to go to heaven. And I don't think we have to worship like we've always worshipped to move ahead. Usually, when you move ahead in God, it is because you chose to walk in a new arena, in a new light. I see things differently, and there's a new understanding, something different going on in me. I used to care what people think. Now, it doesn't matter. I don't even care *if* they think. I'm interested in knowing if what I believe and what I perceive is the true Christ. And if it isn't, I'm asking the Lord to change me.

Have you ever had a car whose timing is off? I've had eight cylinders that ran like six and it isn't a very fun ride. I know some Pentecostals who are supposed to be twelve cylinders, but are running off four. When I'm sick in my body and troubled, I need to know somebody is standing beside me believing that the Spirit will minister to my spirit and give me the strength to stand. Those things don't happen if there isn't true worship going on inside. Did you know you don't have to make noise to worship? We've governed people's worship for so long we believe if you're not shouting, running the aisles and jumping over the pews then---praise God---you're dead. Says who? There are people from whom you never hear so much as a peep, but who are full of the power of the Spirit, and who perceive and understand correctly what God is doing. Those people are the cornerstone of any ministry. And we need more cornerstones. This is where the rubber meets the road.

When I lived at home and showed up at five minutes after midnight, I knew where the rubber met the road. It was wherever I met up with Pop. As a teenager, your Pop doesn't have to come find you but one time before you understand. I've been praying, "God, if You can find us just one time, I believe we'd understand this thing. Lord, wash away all the junk and the ill perceptions. Wash, cleanse, and purify us, and let us be the holy people You've designed us to be." Remember David's words in Psalm 34:1. "I will bless the Lord at all times: His praise shall continually be in my mouth." David was saying that even when he's holding a conversation, in his heart and in his spirit, he's still praising the Lord. In fact, when you see things you don't like and when you are experiencing things you don't understand, let the praises from deep within rise up, and you will begin to speak the truth.

TRUTH FLOWS OUT

Where there is true praise from the inner man, truth begins to flow. Some of the greatest messages that have ever come through my lips have been when I was alone, speaking to myself. We all need a time out on the back side of the pasture where the Lord can whop our fanny---just the two of us. We need that. When we come out of the wilderness, we'll be something different. We'll decide to praise God with our whole life---continuously. It doesn't matter whether it's a good day or a bad day or whether you have a friend or not. It doesn't matter if the church likes you or despises you, if you have a dollar in your pocket or not. It simply doesn't matter, because we're going to praise God with our whole heart---all the time.

BIBLICAL BOASTING

Now verse two of Psalm 34 says, "My soul shall make her boast in the Lord: the humble shall hear thereof, and be glad." We're all prone to boast and often on very slender grounds. I remember, as a young married man, my family would get together in Lake City. Some of the uncles would bring big wads of money. And I loved it, as a young man, when I could bring a big old wad, too. Only it didn't last. Dog rich on Friday, and dog broke on Saturday.

We are to glory in the Lord, not our own goodness. It says, "my soul." Any time the Word talks about the soul, it has to do with direct communication, with your soul making conversation with the Holy Spirit. The Word says, "God is a Spirit: and they that worship him must worship him in spirit and in truth" (John 4:24). It doesn't say in word and deed, does it? No, it means His Spirit talking to my spirit. Remember, Psalm 34:2 shows us in whom we should boast. "My soul shall make her boast in the Lord." Rightful boasting includes the elevation of joyous feeling and breaking forth of gratitude and praise. The best way I can understand what's being said here is to compare it to a football game. You're sitting up in the stadium watching the game, and suddenly, they hike the ball. The quarterback throws the ball to the receiver, and he receives it and breaks out in a run toward the goal. That's how we're to respond---to break out in praise. When you understand what God means to you and when something strikes your spirit, it causes you to break forth in praise.

One Sunday night, there was a young man in our church who didn't understand worship. The music was playing, there was a little bit of preaching here and there, and the Lord was doing His thing like He does so wonderfully. All of a sudden, that young man broke loose in praise, and a few moments later, he was speaking in a heavenly language. I'm telling you, when you get your mind off what is wrong and get your heart on what is right---you break forth in praise. Think back to when God saved you out of a life of sin and when you had no hope, no peace, and no joy. You were poorer than a house cat, but Jesus somehow sent someone with a bag of groceries. If you'd think about this, you'd break forth. When you break forth, it puts a dance in your feet, and all of a sudden, you don't care what people think, you don't care how it looks. I know I can't sing, but praise God, He said to make a joyful noise. He's the one who gave me the voice I have.

True worship says, "My soul shall make her boast in the Lord: even the humble shall hear thereof and be glad" (Psalm 34:2). It is okay to boast in the Lord. It's okay to make noise. It's okay to celebrate, I've made a decision for my own personal life: ain't no rock going to cry out on my behalf. I'm going to praise Him. I'm going to honor Him. When the Spirit moves on me, I'm going to break forth in praise.

Pentecostal worshippers are to be free in their worship. Suppose your pastor took every person who offered to perform a ministry in the church and governed their role in leadership by the amount of worship they brought forth. How much leadership would there be? Suppose he took the choir and said, "Yes, you can sing, and you can make noise, but you can't sing in the choir if you don't understand how to break forth in praise." How much of a choir would you have?

The Lord loves us too much to leave us the way we are. He's trying to shake us up and wake us up. He's trying to remind you that when you were in the valley, He was the one who stood by you. He's trying to get you to break forth in praise. "And the humble shall hear thereof." In other words, somebody's going to speak out. Since I know somebody's going to break forth in praise, I'd just as soon it be me as anyone else.

SPIRITUAL SADNESS SEEKS SECLUSION

Have you ever seen Pentecostals sitting secluded in the house of God? Mind-boggling, isn't it? They say, "I thought no one knew. I never said a word to anyone." You don't have to. Your actions tell it all. What do you think is going to happen when we get to glory? Do you think there are going to be 50 billion seats for people just to sit there?

What is this life all about? Get all the money you can, and crook all you can crook? No, that isn't what it's for. It's to accept Christ and bring others into the fold. And secondly, it is to break forth, to show the world there is a Christ. He is alive. The Pharisees said, "Lord, tell them to hold their peace." He said He could tell them to hold their peace, but they'd seen so many mighty works, they couldn't hold then peace, for it they did, the rocks would cry out. It isn't about money. I thank God for the singers and the choir and the musicians, but that isn't what it's all about, either. Thank God for preachers, but it's about more than that. It's about understanding where He brought us from, and what we've gone through to get to where we are. It's understanding that He loves us the way we are. But He also loves us too much to leave us that way. I have to be willing to walk through another valley to see another mountain. And when I get on that mountain, I'm going to break forth in praise. I'm coming alive. I didn't say I was coming to be a fanatic, but I want true worship.

God is moving. He's saving the lost and filling those who are eager and hungry for the baptism of the Holy

Spirit. He's healing broken homes and causing people to get right with Him. You can't put a value on that. Imagine spending years of your life in prison. All of a sudden, the gate is opened and you hear, "Go forth. Show yourself." Can you imagine being handicapped, physically broken, and all of a sudden health returns? Go show yourself. Go break forth in praise. Show someone the mighty works of the Almighty. What do you think that prisoner's going to do after being locked up for twenty years? He's going to let someone know he made it. It was rough, but he lived through it. It was dark, miserable and lonely. It was a time without family, without hope, but praise God---he made it.

Some of us show ourselves, but it's the wrong kind of showing. Go forth and show what the Almighty has done. The effect of this knowledge should be to make us glad. Does the Bible say to be cold to those who rejoice? No. We're told to rejoice with those who rejoice, and weep with those who weep (Romans 12:15). When somebody comes out of prison, the place where he was bound, I should be standing at the gate, saying, "You made it, go forth and show yourself. That's what the Lord was saying to the Pharisees. The disciples had too much to tell others about to keep silent.

We don't know how to rejoice with those who rejoice or to mourn with those who mourn. About eight or nine years ago, I spent 23 days waiting for my wife to decide if she was going to leave me. I was headlong in the ministry, but my own family was ready to walk out. Why? Because I didn't know how to rejoice as she would rejoice, and I didn't know how to mourn as she was mourning. It took

23 days of not knowing for me to decide to rejoice. I don't care if she rejoices over a butterfly on the wall; I'm going to act like it's the happiest day of my life. Too many of us don't realize what we have until it's gone. I don't care if she mourns over the moon coming up; I'm going to mourn with her. 'Cause I'd rather mourn with her over small stuff than be without her. We have to clear out all this crazy thinking and break forth.

We have had people from other denominations come to our church and say, "I don't know what I'm feeling, but it's awesome." Every person I've ever talked to who has truly gone out in the Spirit gives a different definition, of what they feel. It's something words can't explain.

The Lee University Singers appeared a few years ago at one of the largest Baptist churches in Cleveland, Tennessee, and the Holy Spirit broke out. You just don't ask full-blown Pentecostals to come and expect them not to be what they stand for. That pastor said, "In the 70s, when revival broke out, we Baptists missed it. But let me tell the Pentecostals something, when it breaks this time, we're going to be in the middle of it. They're going to have to move over, cause we're coming through. We're not backing off. We're not going to sit back and be the inquisitive ones, we're going to get out of the boat and into the water. When Jesus says, 'Come,' we're going to come to Him. When Jesus says, 'break forth in praise,' we're not going to ask questions about what we should say, or how to do it. We're going to disregard everything we've ever been taught and truly break forth and show ourselves."

God is saying something, and God is doing something. The effect of this knowledge should make us glad. We have this idea that the Lord's followers are supposed to be melancholy and moppish, to be quiet and discreet. But we have a thousand sources of joy others know not of. There are things to shout about and qualities here you've never been able to experience. That's what the Word is telling us. Every day, every moment, praises shall flow. We must glorify God and God alone. What can better become we who are the creatures of God than to bless Him and depend on Him? What can better become us as Christians than to praise and magnify our God, to whose grace we owe our salvation and happiness? What greater testimony than to show forth when we should be sad and distraught and broken?

HIDDEN TREASURES

Some of you have hidden treasures, qualities a lot of people know nothing of. You want to know why God keeps people around? Because there are hidden qualities in them. God is about to break forth, and you are about to show yourself in a way that's going to astound you. I prophesy it. You're about to break forth in praise. True Pentecostal worship will cause you to lay down the ways of the world and cause you to pick up the righteousness of what He has instilled in you. He will naturally cause you to show your self. I'm hungry for it. God is an awesome God.

Get your mind off your problems, off what you don't understand, off the way you thought it should be, and submit yourself afresh and anew. Say, "Here I am, Lord. Show me what I've been missing." Some of you who have never had a desire to break forth are going to do it now. Submit yourself to the Almighty. I don't care if He has to move in a way I've never known before; I want Him to move. I don't care if He causes me to do and say things I've never known before, let me do them and say them. Let us be a people who will look back and see from where God brought us. Ask Him for boldness to respond to what He's speaking in your life. Ask Him to transform you by the renewing of your mind.

Take a moment to worship Him. As you worship, He will change who you are. He'll help you quit saying things you shouldn't say and thinking things you shouldn't think. He'll help you consider those around you more than you consider yourself. Our God is awesome. Just as much as you have a desire to show yourself to Him, He wants to show Himself to you. He's going to help you break forth. Every day, let praise spring forth.

CHAPTER FIVE

GIVING BACK

We serve an awesome God. He can send a rank sinner to bless you because He uses the foolish things to confound the wise. He takes those who are unrighteous in His sight and uses them to store up to give to those who are righteous. In other words, He will make a way where there is no way. Some have a hard time breaking through that thought, but the way that you break through is to get lost in worship.

Pentecostal worship started in the upper room when there was total unity in the house. From that day to this, Pentecost is flowing throughout the ends of the earth. We are right in the midst of the flowing of that Spirit. God would be satisfied if we just sat there, because He is a gracious and merciful God. But He would be honored if we take the Word out of our heads, place it in our hearts and then respond.

Do you understand what makes a person get up out of a wheelchair and walk? It isn't the man of God; it is the Spirit of God flowing through the men and women of God. Suppose God is depending on your worship to touch some-one's life, to bring healing to them. It only takes one person, but suppose God searched all over and couldn't find one who was willing to worship?

We talk about Sunday morning traditions---give me three songs and a twenty-minute message, a simple prayer, and let me get home before the stew burns. *That's tradition.* Tradition is when you already know what the man of God is going to say, so you click him off and count the seconds. Tradition is where you can just about guess which three out of the five songs you are going to hear. There are church-hurt people out there who have been so trained about worship, they don't have a clue what it is to feel and experience the sovereignty of God. Our God is fighting battles on our behalf.

IS GOD IN THE HOUSE?

It is time for the church to recognize when the Lord is in the house. How many times has He come in by His Spirit and sat by you during a service---and you didn't have a clue He was there? How many times has He knocked on the front door of your heart? We know we don't want Him to show up at the house because of what He will see. When the Lord went to pray, He said to His friends, "My heart is heavy and I need you." His friends couldn't do anything but sleep. How many times has the Spirit of God said, "I'm lonely for your worship, I'm hungry to hear you exhort My Name"?

God is here to meet your need, take care of your problem, dig deep into the soul, and take out the things that need to be taken out. He never takes anything out without putting something else in. He won't put something in that will hurt you; He will only help you. It's amazing how we get in our automobiles and carry on life as usual, ignoring the fact that His Word says, "Teaching them to observe all things whatsoever I have commanded you: and, lo, I am with you alway, even unto the end of the world" (Matthew 28:20). That means no matter where you go, what you do, what's coming out of your mouth, or what you are watching, the Lord is with you. He isn't there to judge you; He's there hoping you will have enough willpower to worship Him. God wants to be worshipped.

Jesus told His followers---and this applies to us today---that when they went in His name and stood according to His Word, He would be there in their midst (see Matthew 18:20). In the passage in Luke, the people were praising God, and then what happened? Understand that anytime God begins to do something, a Pharisee is going to show up. There are always going to be people who come in the Name of the Lord and can quote the Scriptures better than God Himself, but in their hearts, they're nothing more than Pharisees. They are users; they are whoremongers of the Word of God. Show me a man who goes out and does harm in the Name of the Most High, and there you have a man who doesn't understand sovereignty.

I fear God enough that I would never play games or twist His Scripture to fit my needs. Anytime Jesus comes through, there's going to be a Pharisee in the crowd. Some one's going to be sitting there, saying, "I wish he would just hush his mouth." Isn't it amazing that, even though the Pharisees didn't believe in Christ, they still acknowledged Him as Master? I like it when people who don't even like me, still have to honor me for who I am in

Christ. "Ye are of God, little children, and have overcome them: because greater is he that is in you, than he that is in the world" (1 John 4:4). That's why it is important to walk in the Spirit. When you are speaking, be sure it is God who is speaking, because sometimes the Pharisees come to mess things up. They wanted the disciples to shut their mouths, but Jesus said they had already seen so many of His mighty works that if He told them to hush, the rocks would cry out. In other words, there was a fire inside them. They had seen too much to turn back. How many times have we said, "I'll never sing again, I'll never preach again, I'll never teach again"? But in Jeremiah 20 verse 9, the Prophet Jeremiah says,

> *"Then I said, I will not make mention of him, nor speak any more in his name. But his word was in mine heart as a burning fire shut up in my bones, and I was weary with forbearing, and I could not stay."*

You've already seen too much. When God gets ready to dump His bucket of love, you're going to get up, and you are going to move.

BACK TO THE BASICS

God started the Church the way He wanted it, and now He wants it back, the way it was at the beginning. He is tired of complacent churches. He has tried to get through the Pentecostal movement, but some are so set in their ways, they don't want to change. Life is all about change. Ten years ago, I could run around the block;

tonight, I need oxygen to get to the mailbox. Ten years ago, I didn't have gray hair; now that's about all I have. Ten years ago, some of you had hair---now look.

I believe with all my heart that God is taking people from different beliefs and bringing them together to build His Church. He is building the new-millennium Church that will sweep across America, and change and prepare this world for the coming of Jesus Christ. It isn't important that everyone believes like I believe. What is important is our willingness for God to change us. There isn't any way I can say, "I'm going to be the man of God, I'm going to be the preacher of the hour---but God, You're not going to change me." God is in the changing business, so we'd better get used to it. There's a process going on. He is changing each and every one of us and He is building the church. Psalm 34:1-10 says,

I will bless the Lord at all times: his praise shall continually be in my mouth. My soul shall make her boast in the Lord: the humble shall hear thereof, and be glad. O magnify the Lord with me, and let us exalt his name together. I sought the Lord, and He heard me, and delivered me from all my fears. They looked unto him, and were lightened; and their faces were not ashamed. This poor man cried, and the Lord heard him, and saved him out of all his troubles. The angel of the Lord encampeth around them that fear him, and delivereth them. O taste and see that the Lord is good blessed is the man that trusteth in him. O fear the Lord, ye his saints: for there is no want to them that fear him. The young lions do lack, and suffer hunger; int they that seek the Lord shall not want any good thing.

SOUL CONCENTRATION

There is no praise without concentration of the soul. If you want to be distracted, look around. But if you are going to serve God, then be willing to stand and be a man of God and a woman of God. If you are going to run your mouth about the gospel, when the going gets tough, be the last one standing if that's what it takes. Let praise come forth. Jesus said,

> *The thief cometh not, but for to steal, and to kill, and to destroy: I am come that they might have life, and that they might have it more abundantly (John 10:10).*

It's constant. It's the kind of praise that exalts Him. It means you are not ashamed, you are not afraid. Someone out there in darkness needs to hear that you are not ashamed of the God you serve, but that He is worthy to be praised.

He's letting you live; He's letting you breathe His air. Maybe He ought to take you out and put a rock there. You may think this is foolish, but don't you think God can take a rock and put eyes, and a nose, and a mouth on it and breathe life into it? If He can do that to dust, a rock is a whole lot more to work with than dust. It's a sobering thought, isn't it? Can you believe He took a rib and made a woman? Think about the awesomeness of this One we are supposed to be excited about. He said, "This ole' boy is all alone and it isn't good for him to be alone, so I'm going to cause a deep sleep to come on him." I say, "God, put a deep sleep on us and let us wake up in the Spirit." Let us go out in the flesh and wake up in the Spirit. If we want revival to break out, let God cause every one of us to wake up in the Spirit.

Some of you don't want people to come to church with you because of the way you act at work. Before you eat a hamburger after church, try bowing your head and praying about what God has blessed you with. That would be a massive change for some of us Pentecostals. Why should we praise Him? Because there is constant protection. Psalm 34:7 tells us that, "The angel of the Lord encampeth round about them that fear Him, and delivereth them." That means He hangs out around them.

I acknowledge I am not perfect and there are flaws in my life, but I fear Him with my life. I know I was "fearfully and wonderfully made" (Psalm 139:14), and He is doing a marvelous thing. Because of that understanding, His angels are all around me. The Angel of the Lord encampeth all about me. When I'm in my truck, I don't have room for you because the angel of the Lord is there. When I get home, the angel of God is there. Close your eyes, and open your spirit, and you will see angels flying around the room. God will send His Holy Ghost to encamp round about us. Some of us can't see because we are so tied up listening to words.

We can't be what we have always been. Some of you are miserable because you have not been worshipping the way you feel in your spirit you need to worship. Quit suffering and go somewhere where there is freedom to worship. It's time for those who are hungry and thirsty to get in a place where they shall be filled. It is time to think about where He brought you from, and what He has already done. Quit worrying about tomorrow; we don't even have a promise for tomorrow. But thank God we have praises.

A man in our church had a brain tumor as a boy, but tonight he doesn't have a tumor. The devil said, "He has a gift and a talent and I'm going to take him out," but God said "Hold it---he is Mine." Why did he have to suffer that as a young man? Why do we go through valleys? Because years later, we can stand as a cornerstone. When the preacher says, "God can divinely heal you," we know what he's talking about. I sought the Lord and He found me, healed me, delivered me. God gives us the freedom and the understanding.

Don't wait for God to single you out. Be an open vessel, willing to hear. When you are in a meeting, and He is trying to exert you to get up and worship Him, He is going to bless and honor you and take you to a new place in Him.

Righteous boasting includes the elevation of joyous feeling and the breaking forth of gratitude and praise. What are you doing when all that noise is going on? We remember from where He brought us. I was going through the valley of the shadow of death; they served my papers, served my notice, but guess what I remembered? I remembered the day my mind seemingly left me, and Jesus Himself said, "It's okay, son, here's your mind." And the humble shall hear thereof. You had better praise

Him for the mighty works He has wrought in your life, or someone else is going to steal your praise. If you don't praise Him, someone else is going to praise Him.

Some of you say it isn't in your nature to make noise, but you scream and yell while you watch the football game. Then you come into the house of God so hoarse you can't even say hello, saying, "I don't have it in me." That's because you gave it all to the world. You need to take back what the devil has stolen from you. Spiritual sadness seeks seclusion, but not so with freedom and joy. They are like the return of health and sunshine. They say to the prisoner, "Go forth, tell those who are in darkness, show yourselves."

Some of you have been in spiritual prison. God has given you gifts and talents and abilities that aren't based on education or on whom you know, but based on what Almighty God has instilled in your spirit. He said, "Come forth and show yourself."

You see, when the Holy Ghost comes, something has to happen. I've been praying, "Lord, some of them are curious, but don't let them sleep until they come out of bondage. Let them be set free. Lord, let them remember where You brought them from."

EXCELLENT EXAMPLES

Look at the examples of excellent persons. Jeremiah 9:23-24 says,

> *Thus saith the LORD, Let not the wise man glory in his wisdom, neither let the mighty man glory in his*

might, let not the rich man glory in his riches: But let him that glorieth glory in this, that be understand and knoweth me, that I am the LORD which exercise lovingkindness, judgment, and righteousness, in the earth: for in these things I delight, saith the LORD.

Then, in I Corinthians 1:29-31 we read,

That no flesh should glory in His presence. But of Him are ye in Christ Jesus, who of God is made unto wisdom, and righteousness, and sanctification, and redemption: That, according as it is written. He that glorieth, let him glory in the Lord.

Paul was an eminent example of his own doctrine, for when he went to vindicate himself, he found himself obliged to recount what he had done and suffered in the cause of Christianity. Together with his endowments, graces, and privileges, he begs pardon for it, and calls it the foolishness of boasting. Paul didn't want to talk about himself, but in order to exalt the name of the Lord, he was willing to boast and say, "Hey, look what I went through. Look what I've suffered and look how the enemy came to take me out. Yet I stand in awe of the mighty God."

In my own life, thirty-two years ago, I had leukemia---but it was conquered. Fifteen years ago, a nervous condition---conquered. Eight years ago, bankruptcy---conquered. Over fifteen years ago, my daughter was diagnosed with asthma, but today, there's no asthma in her life.

Eight years ago, my daughter suffered chemical burns on her legs in a hot tub. It looked like her skin was going to burst. I called the hospital, and they said we needed to get her there right away. When my wife asked what I was doing, I told her I'd called the hospital. When she asked what they said, I suddenly remembered the nervous condition, the asthma, the broken home, and the leukemia. "They said we need to pray." And together in that room as a family, we prayed and sought God. Immediately after-wards, I began to slap those legs and ask, "Baby, where is the pain?" She said, "Daddy, I don't have any pain." "Baby, are you sure?"

There is a reason to break forth. There is a reason to shout. Think about where He brought you from. Here's what I'm trying to say to you: we're trying to be Pentecostal when all we have to do is respond to what God has done in our lives. Some of you have been listening to the doctor's report for too long. You've been allowing the enemy to cause you to hold back, but you need to get loose in the Spirit. Remember where He brought you from and praise Him.

CHAPTER SIX

GOD'S PRAISE CONCERT

P salm 34, verses 3-6 have a lot to say about praise:

Oh magnify the LORD with me, and let us exalt His name together. I sought the LORD and He heard me, and delivered me from all my fears. They looked unto Him and were lightened: their faces were not ashamed. This poor man cried, and the LORD heard him, and saved him out of all his troubles.

Did you notice how, in verses four, five and six, there are three different instances when someone sought the Lord? There are three different testimonies. In verse four, the writer says, "I sought the LORD and He heard me." Verse five says, "They looked upon Him." That means someone was in distress, someone needed Almighty God to move. Maybe it was a family, a church, a congregation---or maybe it was someone bound by drugs, and the family looked unto Him and was lightened. This is where most of us probably feel we live. This poor man cried, and the LORD heard him and saved him out of all his troubles. This tells me it doesn't matter who you are, what you are going through now, or what you've gone through before. It doesn't matter if your family is together or apart, if you have a good job or a bad one, if you live in the White House or the doghouse. If you cry out to Almighty God, He will uplift you, enlighten you, and encourage you. Seek the Lord, no matter who or what you are, or where you come from, and you will find that He's faithful and just.

Now, it's interesting what the writer says in verse three. No matter where we come from or what we know or do not know, the Word of God exhorts us here. "Oh magnify the LORD with me, let us exalt His name together." That means we should exalt Him no matter what we are facing this week. Are you dealing with problems? We could have a pow-wow and I could match my problems with yours. You know how kids get together and say, "Well, *my daddy* did *this*," and the other says, "Well, *my* daddy did *that*," and "Well, you should *see my* daddy!"? Somebody is going to get the last word. But here, the Word is exhorting us to come together as one, as though we were expecting that upper room experience---expecting something great to happen. The Word says, "Let us magnify the Lord." Don't try to be Him, condemn Him or question Him. Magnify Him. If I were writing on marriage, I'd ask you why you don't magnify those you are living with, and tell them how great they are. "Well," you say, "they are not so great to be with." Then why are you living with them? Either God sent you the one you are with, or He didn't. But if He has given you a marriage partner, treat him or her like a king or queen. "Oh magnify the LORD with me. Let us exalt Him together."

You see, God's praises sound best in concert. One of the reasons I enjoy our denomination's annual camp meeting is that you seldom get five thousand disgruntled believers together. What you really have is what many classify as the cream of the crop. Anyone who makes an effort, in the heat of summer, to go to a place called Wimauma, Florida, is there for a reason. You think lightning pops in central Florida; you should go there. You think there are thunderous storms where you live; you should be there in a storm. You better make sure you are saved. But you have people who come there with one thing in mind to---magnify and exalt the Lord. That is why it is called camp meeting. They want to hear the Word. They don't want to hear what you are going through, what you have gone through, and what your preacher did last year. They want to hear a fresh Word. They want to worship and hear a new song. At camp meeting, people come together as one-just like they did in the upper room.

God is bringing us to new levels. As a rock becomes a solid foundation, we are deeper in Christ---which means we can walk higher in Him. God is taking those who are willing to a new level. As we learn how to be Pentecostal, how to shout, and how to worship differently, it doesn't make us wrong. It just means we're different. If I choose to dance, shout the walls down, and jump the pews---that is my prerogative. That is my freedom in the Lord. And if you choose to sit still and weep before the Lord, that is your choice; it doesn't make you wrong. Pentecostals often give the impression that if you don't shout, you are not saved. That's why many people don't want anything to do with the Pentecostal movement. We have to shut those false mouths, and expose the lies. I'm glad everyone doesn't worship the way I sometimes worship. But as long as worship is of God, there is unity. In worship, some praise with a loud voice, some clap their hands, some dance, some run, and some lay before Him. Pentecostal worship is about freedom in worship.

Do you really think the people in the upper room all acted the same? I don't think so, because we are all differ- ent. Your personality is different from mine. You might be able to sit in church and say, "Lord, I love you," and walk out full, while I might have to get up and run the aisles to feel like I'm full. The key is following the leading of the Holy Spirit. We may worship differently, but that doesn't make us wrong.

Some of us have lived that falsehood for forty or fifty years. I lived it for many years of my life. Sometimes the preacher didn't preach, but I'd go home and say, "We had church." How can you say you had church when the Word didn't go forth? There comes a time that you have to exercise what you have been taught, so there will be those services where all you do is shout. But as a rule, we're not just going to shout fifteen days out of the month. What does it say to a person who doesn't understand?

Our God is a universal God. While He's saving one person out of a life of sin, He may be healing cancer out of someone else, and at the same time, He may be pulling a broken home together. That is the kind of God we serve. And while all this is happening, Psalm 107:20 may be going forth. "He sent his word, and healed them, and delivered them from their destructions." God may be speaking life into some husband or wife, and at the same time be standing and fighting the devil himself on our behalf. That is why we have to speak a univer- sal language---to come together and magnify the Lord. The Bible didn't say to come and magnify the preacher. It didn't say to magnify the nice-looking building. It didn't say magnify each other. But when we come together, we magnify One---the Lord Jesus Christ. And as we magnify Him, it becomes a concert of praise.

I can go down the road by myself and praise the Lord, and certain things will come to mind. I can go to a service where there is a concerted effort to praise Him, and hear someone else praising and thanking God for things on a level I have never experienced, and it begins to draw a new level of praise out of me. I used to sit in the pew and say, "God, when You put the shout on me, I'll get up and move." For thirty-something years, I sat there, never understanding that when you get lost in unified and glorified praise and worship, the Holy Spirit works on you. That's why the idea of Pentecostal worship is going to revolutionize every life it touches. I'm deter- mined that we are going to new levels and new heights and are going to get deeper in Him than we have ever experienced. But we have to be unified.

The psalmist says, "Oh come with me. Oh magnify the LORD. Let us worship the Almighty God as one. Let us make a concerted effort." Wouldn't it be boring if we all stood together and raised our hands the same way, the same time, at the same level, and said the same thing? Wouldn't that be the same thing as some of us are doing right now? But when we come together, we are like an orchestra. Each person has a different gift, a different talent. Each person is a different instrument, if you will. This person can say, "Amen," and this one, "AMEN!" But when you put it all together in a concerted effort, the devil himself has to look around and say, "Wow!" When people are unified, it is awesome. When a group comes together and starts honoring the Lord of Lords, the King of Kings, the Great Messiah, the Great Jehovah, and begins to worship Him in spirit and in truth, awesome things begin to happen in people's lives. The Scripture is saying that we are like a band, so let's come together as one.

IS HE OR ISN'T HE?

Either God is who He says He is, or He is not. Either He is a sovereign God, or He isn't. Either we are full of the Holy Ghost, or we are not.

Behold, I give unto you power to tread on serpents and scorpions, and over all the power of the enemy: and nothing shall by any means hurt you (Luke 10:19).

We either have that power, or we don't.

Every place whereon the soles of your feet shall tread shall be yours: from the wilderness and Lebanon, from the river, the river Euphrates, even unto the uttermost sea shall your coast be (Deuteronomy 11:24).

That is either true, or it isn't. If it is a farce, I'm going to get a job with a tractor that doesn't talk back, or call me at two o'clock in the morning.

God's people need to come together and say, "Oh magnify the Lord with me, and let us exalt His Holy Name together." When we exalt the Master together, the heavenly host goes out before us and begins to fight off things. All we have to do is dance and shout and praise Him, because He said this fight was His fight. That kind of faith comes by knowing and understanding who you are in the Lord. Some of you wish you knew who you were, wish you understood what kind of power and anointing you have. I won't take someone out behind the barn and whip their fanny, but I have a hunch that when I praise and magnify Him, and exalt His name together with you, the Holy Ghost is going to give a whipping to those who have chosen to come against what God is doing. God is doing things as His people come together. When we come together, united in the faith, worshipping and magnifying Him, He sends out the host and fights on our behalf.

Say this: "No more skinned knuckles." When you know who you are, and that your calling is a sovereign calling, you understand He didn't save you to be lifeless, powerless. The Pharisees said, "Master, would You have them shut their mouths and hush all that noise? Would You tell those disciples to keep it all to themselves?" Jesus said they couldn't, because they had already come through too much, and had already seen too many lives changed.

People of God, you have a right to get locked up in praise. You have the right to get together with your brothers and sisters. Quit worrying about what they have or don't have, and how ugly- or fine-looking they are and say, "God, for whatever reason, You called us together as one to give a concert of praise. Lord, I don't really understand my part, but here it goes." As long as I do my part and they do their part, then we can praise Him together. The Bible says it only takes two or three. If I have to, I can train my little puppy dog to worship in a Pentecostal way. He can already stand on his hind legs, and I don't think it would take too much to get him to shout a little bit. If God can use a rock, He can use a dog. He will use a donkey to speak to you, if He has to. He gave you a mouth, and He gave you a spirit, and He gave you a mind to recognize the things He has brought you from. He is saying that if we don't come together as one, He'll take us out of the way and bring a people together who are going to have the spirit of praise. It isn't the Word that's going to make the difference alone. The Word brings understanding and strength. But it is about the worship of the Word that you have received.

What are they doing in Heaven right now? Are they taking 400-year naps? No, they are praising, honoring, and magnifying Him. The four beasts are flying around, full of eyes, and every one of those eyes is seeing God in a brand new way. They are crying out, "Holy, holy, holy! Lord God Almighty!" Just like that, every time we look at God in the Spirit, we should remember all He has done for us. We should be saying, "Holy, holy, holy! Lord God Almighty! I worship You, and honor You for what You have done in my life." When every person gets locked up in that kind of worship, the Spirit comes. You can look around, and where there were eight people in wheelchairs, something happened. The wheelchairs are empty, and those who were once confined to them now are running around like they never could. When the Spirit comes, and you begin to remember where God has brought you from, you break forth. You break out of that shell, and you break into praise because He called us to an outburst.

THE PENTECOST INSIGNIA

Psalm 34:5-6 appears to suggest that a number of thankful souls were gathered together and each contrib- uted his testimony of the exceeding graciousness of God. They joined in an outburst of united and jubilant praise, which is an insignia of Pentecost. They got together. They had an old man over here who was poor and wretched, and a family over there that was broken, and another one over here who was distraught. How do we know this is for us today? Because it says, in verse four, "I sought the Lord." Not my mama, my daddy, my brother, my preacher, my sister, or my aunt. For once, I recognized who I was. I am somebody, because He lives within me and God doesn't make any junk. I sought the Lord and He heard me. That's the testimony.

We don't know if there were five or five hundred there, but Psalm 34, verse 5 says, "They looked unto Him, and were lightened: and their faces were not ashamed." You will never come together with other believers, unified in praise and worship, and not be lightened. I may be tired as a dog physically, but I can't wait to hear more of what God is saying. They sought Him, confronted Him, petitioned Him, and said, "God, we believe."

Some folks are ashamed to bring a friend to a Sunday service because you never know what might happen. But you know what? You can keep them out or hide them under a basket, put a cloth over their head, or sneak them in on a Wednesday, but you better be careful, because the same God, the same praise, the same Spirit that shows up on Sun-day, is right here on Wednesday. Some of us are just too smart for our own good.

If you really want to touch Christ, give in a benevolent way. When you don't need help, give because someday you're going to need help. Look at Psalm 34:6. Here again is the witness of an inspired and grateful soul. "This poor man cried and the Lord heard him." What was he crying for? He was burdened with fears. How many times do we come together burdened with fears? He didn't go to his mama and daddy, or to the country store, and he didn't go rob a bank. He made God his resource. Either God is the God who fights for us, or it is all a farce.

In Jesus' day, there was a little lady who had spent all she had, had seen all the doctors she could, but was still sick. She wasn't even allowed to be around people. Yet she knew this man Jesus was coming through and she thought, if I could just touch the hem of His garment, I think something will happen (Matthew 9:20). She believed. When your life, your family's life, your ministry or your finances are on the line, it's time to put up or shut up. Do we believe Him or not?

When the true God is in the house, there won't be confusion. The devil himself knows how to come in the house of God and worship, so don't ever be fooled. When the writer said his resource was that he sought the Lord, the seeking was a real business. He put his whole soul into the equation. He had a need, he chose to seek, and he sought the Lord. But here is what separates true worship: a lot of us put our minds into it, but this man put his entire soul. He put God on the line. When God begins to move, the natural man says, "God, it had better be You. I've put both of us out there on the line."

One of the ladies in our church had breast cancer---I'll never forget the night she went out in the Spirit, and said, "I'm burning up, I'm burning up." Before I even realized I'd opened my mouth, I said, "The Holy Ghost is burning out the cancer." And immediately fear gripped me, and I said, "Oh God, it's okay to put You out there on the limb, but I put both of us out there." I have never rejoiced as much as I did when the doctors said that where there had been a mass of lumps, there was now nothing. That is because of the sovereignty of God. When you get locked up in praise and worship, and when you are unified, you quit worrying about whether you worship like somebody else does. Some folks haven't shed a tear in forty years-stop worrying about how they worship. Nine times out of ten, the quiet ones are those that, when they speak, it is to say something profound. Sometimes we should be slow to speak and quick to listen. Some of you have made up your mind to disrespect and discredit what certain other individuals say.

Be careful, because you never know when God might give that individual a word for you. Sometimes He sends individuals to speak into your life. You might be missing blessings and staying in unnecessary bondage because you have allowed yourself to carry stuff around. But the more I learn about God, and the more I learn about true, true, unadulterated worship, the bigger my shoulders get. Sometimes, I feel like I can walk over buildings. That is the new level God is calling you to. If you really expect people to throw their canes down, get out of their wheelchairs, and get saved, then you have to change your attitude. If you are truly covered by His blood, then His angels are encamped all around about you.

People don't understand that as we worship, the anointing increases, and there is a greater power. Understand that the greater the power, the stronger the anointing. If you choose to fight me today, you have to fight my anointing. But because I worship in a greater way, tomorrow I'm stronger in the anointing. Now you have a greater anointing to come against. If all of us really believed that, we would stop fearing and start demanding. I want what is mine, and I want what Satan took. I want it seven times greater, because the Word says if he took it, he is a liar and a thief and he has to give it back (see John 10:10). Quit fearing what people say about you, and get lost in true worship. When you pull up at church, get out of the car with your mind on Christ---not on what everyone else has done. I don't care if you don't like the music; surely something is going to be said that is going to strike your spirit. Get lost in praise, and even though you don't

83

worship like I do, it's okay, just worship. As long as we worship in a concerted effort, God is going to show up, and when God shows up, He changes lives. He'll change your condition. You'll go home and say, "Where did it go?" You didn't even realize He already took it from you.

DETERMINED SEEKING

For the psalmist, the seeking was a real business. He put everything within him into the search. Have you ever noticed the look on a child's face when he's pulling on daddy's coattail? "I sought the LORD and He heard me," the psalmist said. Can you believe it? He heard me. When you worship Him---not for what you need Him to do, but for what you have already seen Him do---the anointing is going to increase. There is a difference. It implies heeding and responding. It says man's seeking was responded to by a sympathetic movement on the part of God, and He delivered him. He doesn't just hear you-He responds to your cry. Like never before, we have a mandate to get lost in praise, to get rid of our differences, to quit judging what we have or don't have, and to thank God we are here. Stand, square your shoulders, and know.

CHAPTER SEVEN

HEAD OR HEART KNOWLEDGE?

G od does not only deal with one aspect of our lives. He deals with every aspect. Look again at Psalm 34. Verse eight says,

> *Oh taste and see that the LORD our God is good. Blessed, [or happy, fortunate, and to be envied) is the man who trusts and takes refuge in Him (Amp.).*

Notice that before it gives you these words, you have to back up to verses four, five and six to understand what the Scripture is saying.

We looked at this Scripture in one light already—now I want to look at it in another light. Verse four says, "I sought the LORD and He heard me." There is a difference in what the head, or the mind, left to itself, thinks about prayer. The common, everyday person knows there is a great God out there, but they haven't heard or seen enough to devote their life to Him. The head discerns only the external. It sees man, the creature, venturing into the presence of Jehovah the Creator and asking just what he may wish for. We've all seen people who, when they get into trouble, come to the house of the Lord and say, "I need." Then, there are those who stand and say, "This is it. I am saved, and I'm not going back to the old way of life. You are going to see me every time the doors are open." And then it is a month of Sundays before you see them darken the doors of the church again.

It's one thing to live with head knowledge---it's another to live with heart knowledge. The Word says, "I sought the LORD, and He heard me." You can't honestly seek the Lord if you do not know Him. We think we know all there is to know about serving the Lord, and we sit for years and years proclaiming we have a great relationship with Him. Some of you have sought the Lord---or are still seeking the Lord---week in and week out, year in and year out, while other people come and receive miracles. Four years later, you're still sitting there, saying, "I'm seeking God; I'm just waiting for Him to dump something out on me."

Do you know one of the reasons it is so hard for some-one to receive the baptism of the Holy Spirit? They are waiting on God to pour something out on them. The Bible says, "Faith without works is dead" (James 2:26). If you say you are seeking God, how are you seeking Him? What are you doing? Isaiah 40:31 talks about those who wait upon the Lord. The Scripture doesn't mean "wait" as in sit down and be lazy. Scriptural waiting means I have made a decision. I know I am right in the Spirit, and I am seeking the Lord. There is a difference between lip service and true waiting. If you are truly seeking the Lord, some-thing is going to happen. I have tried to get away from this Scripture, but God keeps drawing me back to the words: "I sought the Lord." He has been reminding me of people who say they are seeking Him, but are the most miserable people on earth. That isn't what the Scripture says. It doesn't say, "I sought the Lord and am still hurting. I sought the Lord and He hasn't heard me in forty years."

It's a poor testimony when you go out in the community and say, "God heals, God saves, and I've been praying for Him to heal me of my cancer for twenty-nine years. Oh, He's a deliverer." I don't know if I want to go to a church like that. Do you know why people go to bars? Because they know that, in about two hours' time, they can get a fix and feel better about things. It's the same reason people smoke dope. Because, when the stuff works, they don't care what is going on. It takes them away from their problems. Recently, I was in a class where they talked about how, if you started off having one or two beers, pretty soon it would take two or four beers to do what the one and two used to do. And then it would take six or eight to do what the lesser amount would do, and once you got up to twelve beers, you wouldn't get any drunker after the twelve beers you just drank. I'm going to correlate this with our faith. We believers think we are supernatural people, and have supernatural faith, but we never see supernatural things happen. We can seek 'til Jesus comes, but we have to move out into that arena where we can say, "I sought God, He heard me, and He delivered me." There is a difference.

I believe the reason the Lord keeps bringing me back to this passage is because our thinking needs to be awakened. Sometimes we need to allow the Lord to get down deeper in us and move us from saying, "I think so, I hope so," to the place where we say, "I sought the Lord and He heard me."

There is a story about a young man who got saved under John Wesley's ministry. He told Mr. Wesley he'd been hearing that Christians have the power to raise the dead. He wanted to know if that was true. Mr. Wesley told the young man it was the truth. Once Christ was in your heart, and you were full of the Holy Spirit and believed in God's mighty Word, then yes, if you spoke it, things would happen. Back in those days, when someone died, the body was kept in the home for a few days. It is said the young man left the meeting and went from door to door, house to house, until he found a boy who had died two days before. The young man went in and by faith raised that boy back to life. That example didn't have anything to do with how long that young man had served God.

I used to think you couldn't speak in tongues until you were an old man. I thought when I was a young man, I was to keep my mouth shut. Then I realized if I didn't make some noise, no one else would, either. In fact, that is what has been wrong with our churches. They tell me a healthy, successful church is one that averages fifty in attendance. How can we be average and healthy if we can seat eight hundred and only have fifty? How can we, as believers, live with ourselves, if we go out with a Pentecostal message, but when people come in, we can't deliver the goods?

It's the difference between operating out of the mind and operating in the Spirit. When the heart speaks, the mind has to shut its mouth. The heart says, "God saved me out of sin, healed me, and healed my marriage." The heart reminds the mind; therefore, the mind has to hush up and listen. I once sat with a man old enough to be my daddy, and watched tears well up in his eyes. In every service, he would sit and weep, praying that God would heal and deliver people. He shared with me that, many, many years ago, God gave him a healing ministry, "What do I do with that?" he asked. I said, "You get on your feet, and if you feel God calling you to pray with someone, then do it." When you feel ministry happening in your heart, your mind says, "Don't go, they will laugh at you. He healed yesterday, but He might not today. Don't give your money; they're not going to make it anyway." That's the mind.

The heart tells you, "God is in the house," while the mind says, "It's storming and sounds like the walls are going to come pounding in. Let's not be distracted." All the while, the heart is saying, "Seek God with your entire being, with all that is within you. Seek Him based on what He has already done in your life." If you have been saved from a life of sin, that is enough to get faith moving. Verses four through six are a witness of what has already happened. Many Scriptures follow the same structure: if you do this, God will do that. I am ready for God to tell me, "Because you have been faithful, this is what I will now do for you." Sometimes we, as Pentecostal believers, have a sheepish faith. The one giv- ing the witness in Psalms said, "I sought God." He didn't just seek God---he sought Him with his entire life, his entire soul, and God heard him.

How many times have we heard the Lord say something and then done nothing about it? How many times have we heard the Lord tell us to do something, yet stayed home? Are your toes curled right now? You know it is the truth. God speaks to us to do things in the supernatural, but because we are bashful in the spiritual realm, we don't do what He asks. Maybe we weren't in the Spirit, or maybe we were not listening to the sovereign God. In Hebrews 13:5, He said He would never leave us or forsake us. He said we would never walk through a valley He had not already walked through. He didn't say He would go around the fire or flame with us. He said He would go through it (Isaiah 43:2). In Daniel 3:20, the Bible tells us about three Hebrew boys about to be burned for their faith. What do you think would have happened if, at the last moment, they had said, "No way, I'm not going. God, I trust you with my life, but this is it, I'm not going any further with you"? They would have missed all God had in store for them, and what He wanted to do through them.

He wants each one of us to have the kind of faith that, when the enemy comes knocking on our door, we immediately remember where God brought us from and can say, "Satan, you are a liar and a deceiver. I know who you are and you are not welcome here I command you to leave!" Look at our military. Could you imagine if, when the enemy was coming, they said, "Hold it, I need to tie my shoes, go to the bathroom, check on the stew, and then clean my rifle..."? The Bible says,

Preach the word; be instant in season, out of season; reprove, rebuke, exhort with all longsuffering and doctrine (II Timothy 4:2).

It reminds us to be ready all the time, because "... your adversary the devil, as a roaring lion, walketh about, seeking whom he may devour" (I Peter 5:8). Satan doesn't want you to have the kind of faith that immediately seeks God, and then, instantly, God moves. But that is what God wants to do in each one of our lives. Then, when we come together, there is great power. Psalm 34:5 says, "They looked unto Him and were lightened, and their faces were not ashamed." They were in trouble; some were in sin. Today we would say some were bound by addiction, by broken homes, by troubled children, and some were bound by depression. The expectation is that in the moment of their despair, they somehow had faith.

BURY THE TAIL

If a friend called with the news that a doctor told him he had four days to live, would you cry? Would you get your shovel and start digging the hole? People say, "I want to move ahead, but I keep remembering what happened in the past." Dig a hole and bury what happened.

A little boy had a pet cat. He slept with the cat, ate with the cat, went to school with the cat, was always with the cat. Then the cat died, and his mama said, "Bury the cat." He said, "I can't, the cat is my friend." He carried the cat around with him for three or four days, until it started smelling rather strong. Mama said, "You have to bury that cat. You've got to let it go." He finally went out and buried the entire cat, except the tail. Every day, he would go out and flip that tail around, until hair started falling off the tail. Mama said, "You've got to bury that thing all the way."

How many times do we bury everything but the tail? We say we're coming out of sin and not going back-but the only friends we have are at the bar. We're not going to receive any more of those ugly gossip calls-so, instead of staying on the phone six hours a night, we're only going to gossip two hours a night. We're not going to criticize anymore---but we still hang out and listen to what the critics have to say.

We bury everything except the tail. Then we seek God and He doesn't hear us. In fact, He does hear us, but He is waiting for us to get some things sorted out. If I lived according to what everyone said about me, my life would have been over twenty-five years ago. As a young man in the land-clearing business, the older men didn't like me because I was successful. Too often we live our lives by how others see us. We live as Pentecostals, but the tail is still sticking out of the dirt.

God is paralyzing those old ways of thinking, and we have to make decisions. Are we going to go with Him? In our minds, we can talk about how great it is when someone crippled comes in and walks out healed. There comes a time you take a step and say, "I sought God and He heard me and delivered me." There is no limit to God, so I'm ripping down and tearing apart all the limits I have placed on Him. We are big enough in faith by now that we can't keep doing what we have always done. We can't keep going to church, shouting and praising God, and then walking right back out and getting into the same mess. There comes a time when you walk out of it, and stay out of it. "They looked unto Him and they were lightened," the psalmist said. Before that, they were in darkness, in a dilemma. There was frustration and heaviness, but they sought the Lord, and He heard them. We as human beings can get in the way---by the things we say, the way we act, and the way we respond---but the Lord wants us to see the witness in this Scripture.

Verse six says, "This poor man cried and the LORD heard him." That is when you move into the supernatural. I may appear spiritually poor because of what I am going through, but suddenly I remember what God has done. In our churches, we need to stand together, seek God, and God is going to hear and deliver us. What does He deliver us from, anyway? All our fears. Somewhere inside, if we're honest, we all have fear. It's easy to stand up and say, "Praise God that He said 'Fear not' three hundred and sixty five times." He did, but the only way you can understand the significance of those three hundred and sixty five times, is to get in that supernatural place. You have to get in that place where your head thinks, "I think God is there. I think we can make it." But while the head thinks, the heart knows. Sometimes, as I deal with the finances at the church, I start looking at the natural. Then someone on our staff will say, "Wait a moment, what are you worried about? Isn't God in this? Pastor, why do you think we are in this valley? So that God can show Himself."

WORTHY OF VALLEYS

When you go through the valley, it is because God counts you worthy to go through it. When God begins something spectacular in your life, He always starts in the night time. Way back in Genesis, chapter one, He said,

> *And the evening and the morning were the first day...*
> *and the evening and the morning were the second day...*
> *and the evening and the morning were the...*

He says, "Weeping may endure for a night, but joy cometh in the morning" (Psalm 30:5). God is always working on you. When you are on the mountaintop and you take a nosedive, understand God is taking you through the valley to bring you to a new place. He is trying to get us to the place, both as individuals and collectively, where we can stand and say, "I've sought God." I wish I had grasped this about four years ago, so that when other pastors looked at our ministry and asked, "How did you do it?" I could have said, "I sought God and He heard me, and delivered me." I believe the reason things don't happen that way is so we don't run around with a haughty spirit and say, "Look at me."

This is all about rearranging the way we think. God moves in different ways. When we get to the place where we think we know everything, it is the first day of our spiritual death. God is a sovereign God. He's going to teach us, and He's always going to increase our faith. You can walk out on Him and turn off your spiritual ear, but the very moment you turn it just a quarter of the way back on, that same voice is going to be there---saying, "I love you the way you are, but I love you too much to leave you the way you are." You either let Him change you now, or He'll be there, waiting, six months from now. You are going to walk through this valley to become what He called you to be, because He predestined you to be with Him before the foundation of the world.

You can't live through the new millennium and act the way you have always acted. There comes a time when we have to say, "No more, no more." It isn't all about crying, but when was the last time you sat in a service and shed a spiritual tear? When was the last time you sat in a service and the Almighty said to you, "Why don't you raise your hands and worship?" It's all about getting out of what we have always done, and getting into something new. I believe this same boredom and complacency is why some of our homes break, why children get on drugs, play with satanic things, and hang out with people we didn't teach them to hang out with. We've let important things slide without realizing it.

A lady came to me for council and said her husband was angry and ready to leave. As she told me how she responded every day when she got home, I was thinking maybe I should go help him pack. But instead, I asked her, "Would you want to go home to you?" She said, "No way, I couldn't stand me." All of a sudden she said, "Maybe there are some things I need to change."

If you have spent twenty years sitting in church, waiting on the preacher to move you, maybe you need to change your thinking. People say they want to hear dynamic preaching. Then go to church in the Spirit, and

God will turn that preacher every which way but loose. "They looked unto Him and His holy presence came and filled the house" (Psalm 34:5).

We have to be the kind of people who seek God on behalf of others. Every person deserves another chance. If we are going to make a difference in people's lives, we have to dig into the Word. We need the kind of power with God that when we seek Him, He hears us right now and delivers right now. Come out of the natural way of thinking---get in the heart of this thing, and let God begin to show you super-natural things. Begin to seek God because you know He hears you and does something about what He hears. David sought the Lord, and the reason he cried out so emphatically is because he was confident God was God. He was confident and put his entire soul into it. "Lord, I'm giving you everything. I'm not going back to the same thing." God knows when we are sincere and when we are not.

God heard David, and came to him. God wants to come to you more than you want Him to come. Think about how badly you want Him to touch you, and multiply that by ten billion times. That is how much He wants to touch you. Everything is surrounded by faith.

I've seen too much. Jesus told the Pharisees, in Luke 19:40, that He could tell the people to be quiet, but they had already seen too much. They couldn't hold their peace---if they did, the rocks would cry out. I've seen too much now to back up. We've come too far to say, "We've made it." We've seen too much to say, "He can't do anymore." Budgets don't matter, bills don't matter, nothing else matters except that we seek God. He hears us and the Almighty moves on our behalf.

CHAPTER EIGHT

REASONABLE PRAYING

Praise ye the Lord. Praise the Lord, O my soul. While I live will I praise the Lord: I will sing praises unto my God while I have any being. Put not your trust in princes, [nor] in the son of man, in whom [there is no help. His breath goeth forth, he returneth to his earth; in that very day his thoughts perish. Happy [is he] that [hath] the God of Jacob for his help, whose hope [is] in the Lord his God: Which made heaven, and earth, the sea, and all that therein [is]: which keepeth truth for ever: Which executeth judgment for the oppressed: which giveth food to the hungry. The Lord looseth the prisoners: The Lord openeth [the eyes of the blind: the Lord raiseth them that are bowed down: the Lord loveth the righteous: The Lord pre-serveth the strangers; he relieveth the fatherless and widow: but the way of the wicked he turneth upside down. The Lord shall reign for ever, [even] thy God, O Zion, unto all gener- ations. Praise ye the Lord (Psalm 146:1-10).

Sometimes we have to look at our spiritual selves and say, "Listen here, soul, shut your mouth about the ways of the world. Get in tune with what Almighty

God has already done in your life and praise Him." In this passage, the writer is talking to himself. He said, "Praise the Lord, Praise the Lord, O my soul." He is saying to himself, "Your life is full of struggle, confusion and pain, but since we are in this frame of mind, praise the Lord, O my soul, because He is all that really matters anyway." Part of understanding how to be a Pentecostal worshipper is understanding how to let the Spirit speak to our spirit. So often our soul-man will speak to our head and say, "Head, tell the soul to praise the Lord." When the devil is messing with you, he talks to your head, hoping he can get to your heart. But there comes a time when you reverse that, and have the heart speak to the head. "Head, shut your mouth. Eyes, stop it. Mouth, listen to what you are saying. Nose, understand what you are smelling, and mouth, tongue, listen and understand what you are tasting. You are tasting the ways of the world, and you need to stop that nonsense and start praising the Lord from within."

Verses one and two remind us to praise the Lord while we have the chance. If you are living and breathing, praise the Lord! Say, "Soul, praise the Lord." Do you ever look in the mirror and say, "You know, you are dumb"? Look at the grandest resolution being stated here: the author's belief in the existence of his soul. One of the greatest lessons we can learn about worshipping God is the soul is what worships the Spirit of God. For those who worship Him must worship in spirit and in truth (John 4:24). The Spirit of God speaks to the spirit of man.

And, as crazy as it sounds, some people believe that when we die, that is it. I'd be disappointed if I thought that. This body is going to die. This old body may be perishing and slowly going down the drain, and back to the earth from whence it came but praise God, I have a soul. I have an inner being, I have a spirit, I have something going on inside me giving me the right to praise my God.

You can't rightfully tell me to shut my mouth and hold my peace, when I've already seen what the Spirit of God has done in people's lives. One of the grandest things you can receive and understand is that when you die, life is not over. It does matter how you live, it does matter if you praise God.

If you knew how important it was to pray and how God does things on behalf of those who pray, some of you wouldn't be sitting in bondage. You would get to church an hour earlier, stay up an hour later, shove the plate back a time or two, just to say, "God, I'm going to take time to pray because the more my soul man communes with Your Spirit, the more things You will work out." I don't know about you, but I have some stuff I need God to protect me from. Have you ever wondered why you didn't give in to temptation when it was staring you right in the face? Some-times it is because your guardian angel stepped in and said, "No. You've been tempted, but your heart would rather fol-low God than enjoy sin for a moment."

Do you know what happens to people who attend four or five churches at one time? It's like serving four or five gods at one time. This one says that, in order to serve

God, you have to sit still and hold your peace. And *that* one says you have to give all your money if you are going to worship God. Another one says not to wear make-up or earrings, but wear long hair and a dress below your ankles, and then another church says, "We don't care what you wear, as long as it is decent. You can stand up and shout, or sit there and keep your mouth shut." Trying to figure out different ministries is like trying to find out which god you want to serve. That is why it is import-ant to get in the Word and understand that you have a soul. When the Bible says, "Choose ye this day whom you will serve" (Joshua 24:15), it wasn't talking about the fleshly man; it was talking about the spirit man. Does that mean I will never be tempted again? No. It means I will probably be tempted more than ever, because I made a spiritual decision that this flesh was going to conform to what my spirit believes in---instead of my spirit con-forming to what my flesh wants. That is why, when you are tempted, you may get right to the point of going overboard, but something will say, "Uh-uh." You may go home a nervous wreck, but the good news is you didn't give in. Why? Because your soul is communing with the very soul of God. There is more to it than outward head knowledge. When you settle for yourself that you have a spiritual soul, you acknowledge the sovereignty of the Almighty.

The body is just a shell, and it either responds to what the head is telling it to respond to, or what the heart is telling it to respond to. The flesh says, "Stay home, I'm tired. I've worked hard, it's okay." The Spirit man says, "This may be the night someone gets up out of the wheelchair. This may be the night a miracle happens. This may be the very service they sing my favorite chorus." The spirit man takes over. At one time or another, many of us have said, "God, if You are out there somewhere... " The very moment I acknowledge there is a soul man, God comes from being way out there, to right here. Then we begin to understand the meaning of Proverbs 18:24: "He is a friend that sticketh closer than a brother." And Hebrews 13:5, "I will never leave you nor forsake you," takes on whole new meaning. Have you ever wondered why He sometimes seems a million miles away? It's because you haven't settled some spiritual things.

A CLOSE-IN GOD

God is not a God of distance. He is a Spirit. And when your spirit settles the fact that there is a spirit in you, His Spirit comes and joins yours. Have you ever wondered why, when you get in a battle, or have an opportunity to witness or minister, you can say things you didn't know you knew? You go home and say, "Wow, where did that come from?" You allowed God to come from way out there, to right here where the rubber meets the road. I don't want a God I can't feel, and I don't want a God I can't find. A lot of people live that way. A lot of people have sat on the church pew for sixty or seventy years with the concept that, every now and then, God is going to pass by. If that is true, then what happens to the Scripture that says He will always be with us? If God said He was never going to leave me or forsake me, if He said He would go through the fire with me, if He was in the furnace with the Hebrew boys, that tells me He is not a God out yonder somewhere. He is a God who is right here, right now.

Can I push your faith to another level? Say this--- "Hello God. It is so good to have You with me today." Now that sounds goofy to the natural mind, but God is a God who will speak to you, and God loves it when you acknowledge that He is there. He loves it when you get out of that mental way of thinking, and realize there is a soul and it's God's soul and God's creation. Even when you don't feel like He is with you, He is with you.

THE SOUL'S DUTY

Look what else the psalmist talks about. Not only does he believe in the existence of his soul, he believes in the duty of his soul to worship. That is why he said "O soul, worship the LORD." He believed he had an obli- gation to worship. People of God, we have an obli- gation. Sometimes we take privileges and act like they are obligations. It is a privilege to give to God, but you don't have to. If you give because you have to, then quit giving, because you are doing it for the wrong reason. If you only tell your companion you love him or her because you feel you have to, then don't say anything. I would rather my wife tell me she loves me once a year because she wants to, than to tell me every day because she feels she has to.

Our soul has an obligation to worship God Almighty. When you worship, the Spirit of the Lord becomes more real---it becomes alive. The more you get out of self and into the soul man, His Spirit communes with your spirit and begins to do things that need to be done in your life. It feels good when the Almighty begins to do something on the inside. The psalmist believed in the duty of his soul to worship. True worship means the whole soul is transported with the sense of His immeasurable love to have your soul following God as the planets follow the sun, drawing from Him harmony of movement, radiance and life.

It is not my head that gets in touch with God; it is my soul man, my spirit. When my spirit communes with His Spirit, my spirit follows after Him, just like when the sun comes up and lights go out. So it is with the soul man. We acknowledge God and say, "At this moment, I don't even feel You, but I know You are there. I have settled it. You said You couldn't leave me, and wouldn't leave me. You said You would always be there. You said if I worship You, You would bless me, touch me, help me, and You would be there." And all the while, He is sitting there saying, "Yes, I said that, and I'm the same God I have always been. I'm a God who cannot lie" (see Psalm 89:35). We serve an awesome God, a God who is true to His Word.

People will try to mess with your head. That is why it is important to know what you believe and why you believe it. People will ask why we worship the Almighty. We must be sure our souls have come to the place of direct communication with God. When my father is out working, and expects me to help him, the dumbest thing I can do is show up and do nothing. It is just as dumb to show up for church knowing God is there, wanting to touch and change lives, and deliver people from sin and bondage, and say, "I don't have a problem tonight, so I'm not going to worship. I don't see God anyhow." We have to rework our thinking.

Have you ever been lost for words when it comes to spiritual matters? Worship is not something we do because we want to; it isn't a choice. We have to. If we want to feel and experience Him, if we want to see Him move through our lives to touch someone else's life, then we have a job to do. That is why the Bible says, "Faith without works is dead" (James 2:20). What are we, the talk of dead faith? A lady once asked me, "Is your church having problems?" I said, "Define problems." She said, "Well, are the people bickering, fussing and fighting?" I said, "No way. Three years ago, yes. Now, they are the most loving bunch of people you have ever seen in your life." That is the truth. There is genuine love. She said, "Okay, then I will consider working with your congregation." She wanted to know if the people realized that it is the soul that matters. Were they in direct communication with the Almighty, or just a bunch of whackos? The soul has an obligation to worship.

The author of Psalm 146 was convinced he must rouse himself to the work. He said, "O my soul." No soul can worship unless it is roused. Man has the power to self-motivate and self-resolve. We cannot be carried up to lofty heights of true devotion. We must climb the rugged slopes ourselves. Ten thousand voices from above are constantly saying to us, "Come up higher." You can't be Pentecostal, be in Christ, be full of the power of the Holy Spirit, have sanctification working in your life, or have a life of praise if all you do is sit there. You *can't*.

The devil doesn't want your mind, your will, your intellect, or your emotions. He goes through all those areas to get at your soul. People say, "The devil is messing with my head and I am going to go crazy." No, you're not. You aren't going to let yourself go crazy, even though the devil may be piercing you and doing his part to get at your soul. The responsibility of your will, emotions, intellect, and all of those areas, is to protect the soul. The devil wants your soul. He could care less if you dress like you are worth fifty million dollars in this life. He could care less what you drive, where you live, what kind of job you have, or how well you sing. It doesn't mean a hill of beans to him. What matters to him is what state your soul is in when you draw your last breath in this life. The enemy's number one job is to get at your soul. He wants to cause another one to lose out, but thank God, we are greater than that.

PAUL'S EXHORTATION

Paul said, "Gentlemen, I wouldn't have you ignorant" (see Romans 1:13). You don't have to be bound, live in dis-guise, be afraid of your gospel, or be ashamed of your God. You don't have to wonder if you are saved. If your soul has accepted Jesus Christ as Lord and Savior, if you die tonight, you are going to wake up in a better place, not a tormented place. I'm talking about the kind of God who said, "I will never leave you." Even when you draw your last breath, He will be there to receive your soul man.

We often pray, "O, God, if I can just make it through this." That is where most of us live. God wants us to under-stand we have the power to do more than just make it. When people ask us how it is going, we should tell them, "It is just awesome!" Every time I look at Him, I see something different. He is awesome. He is saving people, He is changing people; He is filling people with the Holy Ghost. God is awesome. I don't even have words to speak it.

Your soul has an obligation, a responsibility, to worship. I can't rely on my mother's prayers to take me to higher places. I can expect her prayers to protect me because we can pray for each other, but I can't rely on her shout to get me to a better place. We can lift and build each other up, and I thank God for those covenant rela-tionships. That is why the Bible says, "You choose how you are going to believe" (see Joshua 24:15).

When we live our gospel in our heads, we plead, "O, if I can just make it another day." That's head knowledge. But when it gets to be heart knowledge, no matter what we are going through, we can say, "O, it is awesome. I'm making it. I don't like the valley, but I am honored He counts me worthy to walk through it." He said He would go through the valley with me, and when I go through the flame, through the fire, it won't even scorch me. I won't even smell like I've been through fire. He said He was going with us (see Isaiah 43:2).

When you start living this real gospel in a real way, people will want to come, because they are looking for something real. People are tired of spending their money getting high, only to find out when they come down that they are worse off than before. They are ready for a high that lasts a lifetime.

If we worship from our heart, not our head, people will want what we have. They will want what we have found. When they look at us, do we live like what we believe?

CHAPTER NINE

THE CONFIDENCE LEVEL

There are lots of faithful Christians who have faith, but no confidence. The confidence level is what it takes for your miracle. Faith is one level; that is why the Bible says, "Do not cast away your confidence" (Hebrews 10:35). It is easy to let our faith be hampered without understanding it is being hampered. Most of us would say we have faith, but for many of us, it is just head faith. There is head faith, there is heart faith and greater than heart faith, is confidence or supernatural faith. The last thing we need is to let a rock cry out and give God praise and honor in our place.

When Christians come together and give praise, God always shows up. When you get home, God is already there. Is there something in your home you would be ashamed for God to see, or find? Guess what? He is there while you are gone. He sees what is in your automobile. God is everywhere, all the time. He was back at the beginning and He is also at the end. And everywhere in between, God is there. Because of that, it is imperative we understand the importance of praising God. Praise brings the glory down. Even when I don't understand what the doctor said, how I've gotten myself in this condition, or what the preacher is trying to say, God is still there.

Forget where people are from, forget what they are going through, forget who they are just--- understand we all have one purpose. That purpose is to praise Him, honor Him and acknowledge Him. Even now, revival can break out, and somebody can find healing. It doesn't matter where people are from. It doesn't matter what people have dealt with. Some people want to talk about everybody else. If we want to be judges, we can be big-time judges. But being the judge has nothing to do with the soul.

Your soul is like a time bomb, empowered with the virtue, power, knowledge, wisdom, and healing of the Holy Spirit. That is why Isaiah 53:5 says, "with his stripes we are healed." The healing is there. We have already been healed, but what we need is a combination like the woman with the issue of blood. She said, "There is the Healer, there is my miracle. I'm not even supposed to be around people, but I see my Miracle. If I can just get to Him---if I can't do anything but touch the hem of His garment---I believe I will be made whole."

Your soul man is locked up, bound, and packed up with the miracle you need. We have been praying, "O God, come. O Lord, wherever you are." And He has been saying, "Hey, I'm right here." We are not seeking for some God, hoping that He will be touched by what is going on in our lives. Our soul is nothing more than the Spirit and the power of God that is already there.

When you understand you have a soul, you understand that the soul has a responsibility to praise the Lord.

It is time we say, "Soul, I know you are there. The devil has had me blinded and you have been hiding from me. I thought God was out there and all the time He has been inside me, but now that I know, you have to wake up, get up, and start praising."

Why do you think that out of the belly flow rivers of living water (see John 7:38)? So you can dream about a pretty river somewhere? The river is not out there; your river is inside you. You have to wake up your soul. No longer are we looking for God-we are acknowledging God. When virtue, through praise, begins to ooze out, that is your miracle, that is your healing, because sickness, cancer, and disease can't stay where the virtue of the Holy Spirit is. True worship causes virtue to flow out, and sickness has to go in Jesus' Name.

WAKE UP THE SOUL

It is time for us to get up, to wake up our souls. Do you know why the Bible talks about unity? Because we need to understand we have a soul, and a responsibility to praise God. In praise, virtue is released. People want to get to the pastor, saying, "He is anointed and God can heal me." You are already healed. You just have to gain the kind of faith that expects things to happen. That is why we have to talk about confidence. Confidence is taking faith to a higher level. We say we have faith that God is real, we have faith that God is here, and we have faith that we feel something. The real question is whether we have the confidence that what we feel is the real God. We have to get out of the head and into the heart.

Men's bodies are dying; men's purposes are perishing. The great shores of destiny are crowded with the wrecks of purposes that have been broken, with unfulfilled hopes, unrealized plans.

--David Thomas, D.D., *The Biblical Illustrator*

Psalm 146 reminds us that man's dreams can only go so far; men's purposes can only go so far. That is why Galatians 5:16 says, "Walk in the Spirit and you will not fulfill the lusts of the flesh." How many preachers have led peo-ple down a dead road? Proverbs 18:19 tells us that a brother or a sister who has been offended is harder to win than a whole city. Don't put your faith in man.

Several years ago, when we lived in the Ocala National Forest, my nerves were not what they should have been. My wife prayed, my mama prayed, the neigh-bor prayed, everybody prayed. It didn't mean a thing because in my mind, I needed the preacher. When the preacher finally got there, he never even prayed for me and I started feeling better. My mind was set on what man could do, but a few years later, I realized it wasn't man who was my salvation. Man was only someone who could lead, guide, help, and direct me. It wasn't the man who had the power---it was the power in the man. God taught me not to depend on mankind.

God already knows what is wrong, so let's start tell-ing Him what's right. He is a good God, a great God, a faithful God, who cannot lie. He is a sovereign God, the great Physician, the Wheel in the middle of the wheel, and the Lily of the Valley. He already knows what we need, because He is there with what we need. But the more praise is lifted up, the more anointing comes down, and we can only hold so much. That is why Jeremiah said it was like fire shut up in his bones (see Jeremiah 20:9).

When folks from other denominations come to our church and experience free worship, it makes them feel good. If some of you stood up in your services and said, "Lord, I love you," you would get booted out, or told, "We don't do that here." The story is told of an old farmer who joined a church. He would go in there, and shout and praise God, and whoop and holler. The deacons were told by the pastor, "You have got to quiet him down." They said to the farmer, "Sir, we don't do that here." He would settle down and the next Sunday, he would come in and whoop and holler, shouting and praising the Lord. After several weeks, the pastor and the deacons went to the old farmer's house and found him plowing his field. "Sir, we have to tell you: if you can't hold your peace, you will not be welcome in our church, because you are disturbing what God is doing. But we want to know why you always make noise." The old farmer said, "Let me tell you why I can't hold my peace. When I was a little boy, the Sunday school teacher led me through the sinner's prayer. I felt Jesus come into my heart and when I grew to be a young man, and found myself in a place of rebellion, I turned and said, 'Jesus, I know You are there.' Jesus showed up again for me. I remember how I called on the name of Jesus when I asked that little lady to be my wife for life. I remember the hard times, the times we had no food, the times there was no passion and no peace in the home, but Jesus always showed up. He would even send strangers to help us and feed us. I remember the time I was in a little church, and I began to praise God, and the Holy Ghost began to come down. Boys," he said, "hold these reins and let me shout for God for a while." That is the freedom of worshipping God, because it is in the worship that miracles take place.

I remember a worship service where a sister came and stood down front. We prayed for her, and she went down in the Spirit. Then she looked up, bright-eyed, and said, "I am burning." What you don't know is that the doctor's report in her pocket said she had a severe case of breast cancer. When God took her out in the Spirit, that burning sensation was the virtue already in her being let loose. She got up, and when she went back to the doctor, he said, "This report says there is a mass of tissue that shouldn't be there, and this other report says it's gone. I can't believe it is the same picture."

I saw man singing a song that was dear to his heart. His whole face lit up like a light---the light of the Holy Ghost. A bulb lights from the inside out. Jesus said, in Matthew 5:14, "You are the light of the world."

When the soul genuinely begins to worship, virtue begins to flow, and you see people light up. Like a woman who is expecting a baby---even before her pregnancy shows, there is a glow about her. You just know something happy is going on inside. When the Spirit of God begins to flow from within, we light up on the outside. That is why you see people dance, run, lie down, and get into a little skipping fit. It is because something intimate is taking place on the inside.

GO AHEAD, GOD

Some folks tell God, "Go ahead and move me," and then they sit and wait. I would rather watch a car rust than watch God try to move some people. It would be more fun. We have had folks come and say, "I have been watching people get lit up, and I thought it was fake, but now I am learning it is because of the soul's relationship with the Master." That is why Jesus said He dealt every man a measure of faith (see Romans 12:3). He already knew He was going to be inside you. Some of us think we can run and hide---but from whom are we going to run and hide? God is with us, even when we are not living according to the way man says we should live. If the God in us is not bigger than what people see on the outside, then it isn't God calling us. When it is God, we overlook faults. We have a responsibility to arouse the soul and get our eyes off man.

I thank God for doctors, because in part, God chooses to heal through them. Don't ever curse the doctor---thank God for that part of the creation. But don't ever take the doctor's word as the last word, either. It isn't over until God says it is over. It is our job to keep our composure, to arouse the soul and say, "God, I know who You are and I know what You are in me." Once you understand your soul's responsibility, you begin to understand who you are. That is when you get out of faith, and into being confident.

Do I struggle? Yep. Do I get mad? Yep. I have been put out all week. I have had just about all I can take of some things. When we awaken the soul, we hear each other's brokenness and hurt. If, in that hurt, someone says something they shouldn't, you won't even hear the negative. You will know your heart encouraged their heart.

Do you know why a lot of people fall? Loneliness. For years, some have tried to share their hurts with people they thought were friends, and next thing you know, the friend is blabbing it to everyone. So, now, we live in a paranoid society. Many of us have deep-down hurts we are afraid to tell anyone. We are afraid they are going to run their mouths. When you understand who you are and that your soul man is ordained and created by Almighty God, then you understand that the measure of faith is just another way of Him saying, "I have equipped you with an incredible anointing." In I John 4:4, John reminds us that, "Greater is he that is in you, than he that is in the world." What is within me? God, the faith of God, the anointing, and my soul. Is all that is within me in my big toe? No. You can get your big toe cut off. You will have pain and lose your balance, but you can't kill the soul. You can kill the man, but you can't kill the soul, because it is the living, breathing creation of Almighty God.

God has anointed us, and every one of us has an incredible anointing within us. If we want that anointing to begin to come out all over, we need to get lost in praise. When you get up in the morning, instead of saying, "O, God," get up and say, "Hallelujah, praise the Lord!" Every time you say, "Hallelujah," you are building up God's Kingdom and tearing down the devil's. Yes, I am in pain. Yes, I am suffering, yes, I am hurting---but hallelujah, the devil's kingdom is coming down and the Kingdom of God in me is coming up.

THE HAPPIEST CONDITION

We have to learn how to praise Him. We must get our eyes off man. According to verses 5-9 of Psalms 146, the happiest condition is knowing that the God of Jacob is all-powerful, that the God within me is all-powerful. The happiest condition of the soul is to know that the God of Jacob is absolutely truthful and infinitely merciful. Trust in Him who lives forever. You may not know why you are going through the things you are going through, but God is truthful, He is faithful, and He knows what He is doing. He has you in His hand, and is just breathing life into you. He is filling up your reservoir.

When we get into the attitude of praise and sincerity, there is no telling what is going to happen. Some of you may go back to the doctor, no telling what kind of report you will receive. People say, "Well, I didn't feel anything." God didn't say to rely on what you feel. He said you have to live by faith---instead of feelings. That is where you get out of trusting in man and get into trusting God.

A touching story is told of an old Methodist singer, afflicted with cancer on his tongue. At the hospital for an operation, holding up his head, he said, "Wait a bit, Doctor, I have something to say to you." He asked the doctor, "When this is over, shall I ever sing again?" The doctor could not speak---there was a big lump in his throat. He simply shook his head, while tears streamed down the old fellow's face and he trembled convulsively. The sick man then asked the doctor to help him sit up. The man said, "I have had many a good time singing God's praises, but you're telling me I will never sing after this. I have one song to sing, which will be the last. It will be a song of gratitude and praise to God." And then, from the operating table, the old man sang one of the old hymns. "I'll praise my Maker while I have breath."

Get your mind off what is wrong, and get your mind on what is right. While you have breath, arouse the soul to praise: O, praise ye the Lord. O, magnify His Holy Name. While I have breath to breathe-while I have yet a breath to sing-I'm going to sing praise for what He has already done. I'm going to praise Him for all the mighty acts He has done in my life. Let these words fill your reservoir, your soul, with enough faith to say, "I don't know why, but I'm going to praise Him. I don't know why, but I have to glorify Him." Some of you are going to wake up in the middle of the night and say you don't understand. Just praise Him. Activate and let loose what God has placed within.

CHAPTER TEN

PRAISE IN ACTION

W e are often so busy waiting to see what God is going to do next, we forget what He has already done for us. Sometimes, we have to slow down and pick up those miracles, and say, "Oh Jesus, I forgot to praise You way back when. I have been so selfish. God, if You never touch me again, I have nothing I can gripe about." He saved me, sanctified me, and filled me with the Holy Ghost. Time and time again, He has healed my body, my family, my marriage, and my children. He has healed everything there is about me, and even in the midst of this, there are miracles. We have a reason to shout. We have a reason to back up and say, "Lord, let us take time out to praise You for what You have already done."

> Praise ye the LORD: for [it is] good to sing praises unto our God; for [it is] pleasant; [and] praise is comely. The LORD doth build up Jerusalem: he gathereth together the outcasts of Israel. He healeth the broken in heart, and bindeth up their wounds. He telleth the number of the stars; he calleth them all by [their] names. Great [is] our LORD, and of great power: his understanding [is] infinite. The

LORD lifteth up the meek: he casteth the wicked down to the ground. Sing unto the LORD with thanksgiving; sing praise upon the harp unto our God: Who covereth the heaven with clouds, who prepareth rain for the earth, who maketh grass to grow upon the mountains. He giveth to the beast his food, [and] to the young ravens which cry. He delighteth not in the strength of the horse: he taketh not pleasure in the legs of a man. The LORD taketh pleasure in them that fear him, in those that hope in his mercy (Psalm 147:1-11).

I believe that those who are in tune with Him, in the last days, are the people whom God is going to touch. We get in tune with Him when we start giving Him praise. What is praise?

As applied to me, it has a limited use, differing in degree rather than kind, from that which is employed in devotion. It is the expression of pleasure, of approval, of gratification in an action, in a course of action or in the contemplation of one's disposition.

-Henry Ward Beecher, The Biblical Illustrator

Although man should receive some praise, he shouldn't receive too much praise. If we go to church, and all we do is praise each other, then certainly we have left the main factor out. The main factor is the Lord Jesus Christ, because He is the one who suffered, was cursed and bruised, and spit upon, and He is the One who died. He is the Great Physician, the Great Messiah, the One who has made the difference in our lives. He is the One who should receive the praise. It is okay to give praise to man, but it should be limited praise. When you give someone else's family more praise than your own, you are wrong. Some of you get frustrated when other people come and bless your family, and yet you won't bless them. We often give each other praise when we should be giving God the praise. I appreciate it when people say, "Oh, Pastor, you did a great job." Thank you so much, but greater than that, look what Jesus has done. All I can do is speak words to you---Christ, however, can speak into your heart, into your spirit, and can give you the strength and the passion to praise Him.

SPIRITUAL FLASHBACKS

You know what happened in the upper room. They all got in there and took a nap, right? No. Christ's followers got in there and had a praise meeting. I believe at just the right moment, when they---in unison---began to praise Him for something He had already done, they had a flashback. It's time to ask God to give us a flashback of something He has worked in our lives.

I remember a strong man, in good health, who was suddenly diagnosed with cancer. The church prayed and anointed him, and stood by him as only the church could. Today, he is the picture of health. God healed him of cancer. Another lady I know has a great anointing, and I cherish her ministry. I have said, "God, if I can just have a piece of her anointing, that would be great." There was a time when she got out of bed every morning and had to tape her eyelids open. Only when she was preaching or singing would the eyelids stay open. You tell me the anointing isn't powerful. For weeks and months, she suffered and her eyelids got raw because of the tape. But all of a sudden, she was healed. When it happened, I was out riding on my tractor, dust all over me, with tears running down my face. I imagine the neighbors thought I was nuts, and I don't know if it was those tears that caused her miracle to come. When you let loose in praise, you don't know when God is going to use your praise to heal someone else's life. That is why we have to praise Him, why we have to give Him honor, and why we have to open up.

WHAT IS TRUE PRAISE?

It is a knowledge of divine manifestation. It means that when you see where God worked a miracle in someone's life, you have the soul responsibility to get up and shout. We are not here for dictatorship, but we are here to get free in the Spirit. Whatever the Spirit feels should be said out on the airways, that is what the Spirit is going to let come forth. It is no less than dictatorship when you sit there with a miracle and keep it to yourself. Miracles are given to you so you may give them. When you need a healing in your body and you hear of other miracles, it gives you faith and makes your soul full of the anointing, of virtue. That virtue begins to ooze out and becomes, like Jeremiah says, "fire shut up in my bones." If you ask what is going on inside me, I'll tell you it is like a fire.

Praise is not merely the utterance of a feeling of plea-sure, or of gladness welling up in the heart. Some things we do because it feels good, and other things we do because of what we know. Why do you think a child gets you out in public and pulls on your coattail? They know they can get away with it. They know you are not going to whip them. They don't fear your threats, because that is all they are: threats. You know why the devil won't leave you alone? Because all you do is threaten. But it is time to stand and say, "Hold it, I remember when I was in a valley." Do you want to be depressed for the rest of your life, do you want to be sick for the rest of your life, and do you want to suffer for the rest of your life? The answer is, obviously, no. Then you have to praise Him, honor Him, and remember where He has brought you from.

The act of praising implies also a moral taste, which feels and enjoys the noble attributes of God. When you feel a movement of God even when you don't understand what is happening---open your mouth and say, "Lord, I praise You. I don't fully understand it, it is scaring me to death, and I want to walk out the door, but I believe You. I know it wouldn't be my nature to stand and shout, but I feel something on the inside." When you feel Jesus working on the inside, you can't keep Him in. You have to let go. You have to let Him out. Let Jesus out of the bag. It is an overflowing feeling.

This is where Pentecost comes in. It may take place consciously. I go to church with a conscious reason. I want somebody's life to be changed. I am convinced if you hear the Word, receive the Word, mix it with praise and worship, and stir it up with the faith you already have, miracles will happen. Some have walked in bound, but are going to go home loosed.

The highest forms of praise are spontaneous, irresistible and full of interjection. I may be sitting there doing my best to be dignified, just wanting to make it through the service without people looking at me, when the Holy Spirit suddenly shows up. I may be a visitor, and my friends have said if I showed up one time, they wouldn't ask me again. What I don't understand is that if I come even just one time, the Spirit of God will come over me.

Years ago, I had decided I was going to leave our home church and start a youth group at a small church. My wife was scared to death, and I didn't blame her. I went and visited that church, and the same day I made the commitment to go and be the youth pastor, their pastor made a commitment to leave. I thought, what is up with this? At the end of the service, the pastor said, "Folks, I am doing my best to dismiss you, but I can't. Someone needs to say something." God had never used me in that fashion before, so my heart was pounding at the thought of talking to folks old enough to be my mamma and daddy. So I prayed, "Dear Jesus, I don't really think this is You, but if it is, let him ask one more time." At that time, the pastor said, "People, I want to let you go home. I know the stew is cooking, but someone needs to obey the Lord." My heart was pounding way out of my chest. I said, "Jesus, I know You are not talking to me, and I can't say those things to them, but Lord, if it is really You, I mean if it is really You, let him ask one more time." The pastor said, "Folks I'm telling you the truth---I want to let you go, but if I do, I will be disobeying God." And before I realized it, I was up in front of those people speaking my heart to them. How did I know it was God? When I left home, I left an angry wife, but by the time I got back, she met me at the door and said, "What is up with you?" I said, "What do you mean, what is up with me?" She said, "What have you been into? What did you do?" I said, "Who called you?" She said, "Nobody called me. All I know is that you went over there and said something, and I feel God might be in this thing." We both broke down and began to weep as we realized God had spoken to a young man and used him to exhort a group of people to put the hurt of yesterday behind them.

Remember the good times, remember the great times, remember the miracles, and then take those times and begin to step ahead. When God reminds you of something He brought you through, it isn't so you can harbor those feelings. It is so you can share them, because somebody needs to hear about your miracle. Somebody has a miracle in sight. That is why I keep telling people Jesus saved me, healed me, delivered me, and took leukemia out of my blood. When they want to check my blood, I let them peck away. They can take a six-pack if they like, because I know what kind of blood they are going to find. They tell me I have pretty blood; it is because it is Jesus' blood.

The highest form of praise is spontaneous. While you are sitting there, minding your own business, God reminds you of somewhere He has brought you from and you can't help but get up on your feet and praise Him. It won't matter what anybody thinks about you, because what is going on inside you is real. It is something lasting. Some of you need something real to get hold of you. Some of you need something lasting to get hold of you. Some of you have been sitting in the House of God for so long you have become stale. You hear the Word, but it is of no value, and when you don't receive the Word, the Bible says it causes unrest. (see Hebrews 4:2-3). That means the Word is coming in, but you are blocking it. You are keeping it from coming in and doing the work God ordained.

Jesus is alive. Jesus is for real. I thank God for what He is doing in my life. I thank God for what He is doing in your life. If you look at your life, for every reason you should be depressed, I will show you twenty five reasons why you ought to be on your feet shouting and praising---because, if you don't praise Him, the rocks will cry out. I once spoke with a man, and with tears he said, "Pastor, I guess I don't really understand. My life has been surrounded by miracles. I have prayed with people and I have seen miracles happen, but it seems in the last few years there hasn't been a lot going on." I said, "What makes you think you have the gift of healing on your life?" He said, "When I wasn't even saved, an automobile fell on my hand and crushed every bone in it. My hand was wrapped up, and I couldn't even move my fingers inside the wrapping." He told me he went to a little

Pentecostal church that was having a revival. "Not only did I get saved, but before I realized it, something happened. I didn't even know there was a God who healed, but I started moving my hand and the pain left. When I went to the doctor, he took the wrap off, and that hand was whole."

Two weeks later, the man and his wife went to visit their son in North Carolina. The morning after they arrived, the son had a head-on collision with a pick-up truck. He was on a motorcycle. He broke a leg, messed up an arm, and they said every bone in his wrist was like powder. That would make you want to say, "Oh, Jesus." Sometimes we are destined for valley times, and we just have to accept it. But God allowed this couple to be there. The man's wife would have gone crazy if she had to drive all that distance to North Carolina, knowing her son was in intensive care. Now, that boy's hand was crushed, and there was nothing the doctors could do. Except Daddy remembered a miracle from thirty years ago. He sat beside his son, looking at his crushed hand, and what do you think went on in his mind and heart? God, You healed me---You can heal him. God, I know there is a miracle, because I am a miracle.

Why should we praise Him? Jesus wants to touch some-body, and it is real! People might not act the way you think they should act, but never underestimate the power of God in their lives. Jesus is a miracle worker, and there is a reason to shout. I dare you to tell my mother to sit down when she gets to dancing her little dance, because she remembers when the doctors said she was going out---but Jesus said she was coming in. There is a reason to shout. There is a reason to praise Him. Jesus is the only real deal.

THE EVIDENCE OF TRUE FAITH

True praise is evidence of true faith. When you have true faith in the house, anything can happen. Someone can get saved, while someone else gets out of a wheelchair. Some-one can be filled with the Holy Ghost, while someone else is having a blood transfusion from the Holy Ghost. You can come to God stuttering, but when you get right with faith, and when you let faith have its perfect place, then true praise comes. And anytime praise comes, miracles come. They said I was going to die, but I'm alive. It is because Jesus came into my heart. He was bigger than the doctors were. I have a reason to shout. When we can do nothing but say, "God, it is You and me---You are the only one who can make a difference," that is when Jesus comes in.

I'm not talking about something that happened forty years ago. Some of you are so stuck on what happened forty years ago, you couldn't see God if He walked up and kissed you. The devil hates me, and he doesn't like what I stand for. But it is too bad, so sad, because Jesus loves me, Jesus healed me, Jesus delivered me, Jesus has given me a voice. He heals, He delivers, He sets free.

I remember a man standing in a service hurting, his body folded up and in excruciating pain from arthritis. The minister began to rebuke the pain, to rebuke the arthritis, and that man began to tremble and shake. Before it was over, he was on the platform dancing all over the place. Jesus is alive! If you don't praise Him for what He has already done, the rocks are going to cry out. Make a noise---because Jesus inhabits the praise of His people.

CHAPTER ELEVEN

GENUINE WORSHIP

T he other day, a man told me the devil was after him. I said, "Well, stop running." The worst thing you can do when you're facing a bad dog is to turn and run from him. We must not only have faith, we must be confident. I am confident that, no matter what comes against me, I am a blessed individual. And because I am blessed, I am victorious. I've not yet seen a blessed person without the victory. The two simply don't mix.

I looked up "blessed" on my fancy little computer, and it told me over 404 Scriptures refer to being blessed. In the Word of God, I have more than one "blessed" per day to live on. I'm blessed, I'm blessed, I'm blessed, I'm blessed. I'm blessed with good health, I'm blessed with a family, and I'm blessed with a wonderful church. I'm blessed with the joy of the Lord. I'm blessed with money in my pocket and with something decent to ride around in. I'm blessed with clothes on my back. That's a reason to get excited and shout.

But in all of the blessing, something is always going to go wrong. Like it or not, there's always going to be at least one Pharisee hanging around. It only takes one rotten apple to start a big mess. We may go through trials and tribulations, and there may be reproaches that come against us, but praise God, we don't have to live under the bondage of the reproach. We must be confident in who and what we are-and where He's already brought us from. Hebrews chapter 10, verses 32 to 35 says this:

> *But call to remembrance the former days in which after you were illuminated ye endured a great fight of affliction. Partly which ye were made a gazing stock both by reproaches and afflictions and partly which ye became companions of them that were so used. For ye had compassion of me and my bonds and took joyfully the spoiling of your goods. Knowing in yourselves that ye have in heaven a better and enduring substance. Cast not away therefore your confidence which hath great recompense of reward.*

Before you get to the victory, to the great times, you're going to walk through a valley. You might as well get used to it. You're not a bad person because things come against you. You're a blessed person. Verse 32 says, "Ye endured a great fight of affliction." Now, this was written to the believing Hebrews. They were exhorted in the sufferings to which the Apostle refers. The term "affliction" is usually used to denote bodily indisposition, but it is obvious the reference here is to persecution. In other words, as a Christian, you're going to be persecuted, and you're going to go through tough times. This junk some preachers feed people---telling them all they have to do is pray a simple prayer and everything is perfect---is hoopla. It's wrong. It's worse than the stuff you find in a cow pasture. You can't live on it.

WHO ARE YOU LIVING FOR?

The very moment you accept Christ, the devil isn't going to like you. People say, "Pastor, me and the devil ain't never had a problem." That's because you're living for him. As soon as you quit living for him, he's going to have problems with you, and you're going to have problems with him.

The devil doesn't like it that you've given your heart to Jesus, but Jesus Christ loves it. I don't care how dead you feel spiritually---if you have enough God that you can speak God's Holy Name, the devil fears who you are and what you already know. He knows you came from a place of weakness, death, and coldness, to a place where there is life and understanding. There is a greater understanding when the Word says you endured a great fight of affliction. When the Word says you endured, it doesn't mean, "When you're about to go through." It says you've already come through. There is a little baby in our church who, according to the doctors, wasn't supposed to be here. But there's a baby, because God's Word is greater. God's Word is marvelous.

Jesus died so we might have life. He paid the price so we wouldn't have to pay it. He didn't say He was going to take away the pain or the affliction. He said He was going to be the one to pay the price for us. You still have to carry the cross; that's why the Word says they endured a great fight of affliction.

It's okay to go through the valley---it's okay to suffer and to walk through pain. This affliction is not only physical pain, but also bondage in our minds. The Hebrews also dealt with people making fun of them, and telling them their God wasn't real. This is why we have to be in the Spirit, and be sure every song edifies the body of Christ. There are doubters and Pharisees who simply do not under-stand that God is real. The Word says you have endured the great fight of affliction so you may stand and be confident, knowing you are saved. Knowing that He heals. Knowing that He delivers.

A young man, Kevin Richardson, was in an accident. He was told he would have to have more leg surgery. His leg was wrapped up in a cast, and he was crying in pain. Before the surgery, the doctors walked into his room, took the cast off his leg, and said, "It isn't as bad as we thought it was. We're going to send you home." Tell Kevin that God doesn't heal!

Jesus is alive, Jesus is working, and Jesus is making things happen. Tell the sweet little lady who walked into our church on a Tuesday morning that Jesus isn't alive, and see what she says. When she walked in, her ears were plugged up and she wore hearing aids. Those ears popped open, and she took the hearing aids back to the doctor. Tell her Jesus isn't alive, and then tell her the affliction she walked through wasn't worth it. She'll tell you she didn't like the pain, but she wouldn't trade it because she found Jesus in the pain.

I don't like pain. I don't like suffering. But in Hebrews 10:35, the Bible tells me not to cast my confidence away. It's in the tribulations and tough times that you move from faith to confidence. When you move into confidence, that's when you start walking like you're someone.

Jesus is alive! He is the Great Physician, the Great Savior. A lady named sister Thelma Smiley was in the hospital on life support. She was struggling with pneumonia, radiation, chemo, and two heart attacks, back to back. The family was called in and told, "This is it." But tell her that, because ten days later, the doctors took all the tubes out. For two days she breathed on her own before she had difficulty again. Then, the doctors went in, and sucked the most horrible-looking garbage you have ever seen in your life out of her body. Now they say they can't find any cancer. She doesn't need radiation, therapy, or chemo. The heart is fine, and they can't find the pneumonia. Go tell her that walking through the great fight of affliction isn't worth it.

Doctors told a man named Paul, from our church, that his body was eaten up with cancer. He walked into church one week a sick man, and a week later, the doctors said the cancer was one-quarter the size it was before. You couldn't tell him that Jesus isn't real. We have a reason to shout. We have a reason to praise God. We have a reason to build our faith.

REJOICE IN TRIBULATION

The term of our suffering can, at most, be short. This is why we should rejoice in tribulation. We suffer in a righteous cause, to show someone Jesus lives. Even when we're in a place of affliction, there's something to have joy and rejoice over. And if I lose my life, I have a greater place waiting for me.

You can make it to heaven sick as a dog, eaten up with cancer, but you can't make it to heaven without Christ in your heart. We should get our mind off being healed, and ask, "Brother, are you saved? Sister, do you know Jesus?" That is the most important message. True salvation gives me joy and peace and happiness. It helps me rejoice when I don't understand why things are happening. In Isaiah 53:5, God said by His stripes we are healed. Let Him take care of that, and you take care of your salvation.

The Word says if we suffer with Christ, we shall also reign with Him (II Timothy 2:12). Even the prophets, who possessed the Kingdom of Heaven, were persecuted. But great is their reward in heaven. Jesus is waiting for us. He said He was coming back, but while He was gone, He would prepare a place for us. You talk about singing here; wait till we're singing there. When we get to glory, I'm going to join the choir. Let Jesus flow within you, and sing like you've never sung before.

Why do we suffer? Why do we rejoice? We suffer when we're despised and in the minority, and when our doctrines strongly clash with the reigning maxims and controlling interests. The Hebrews suffered, and rejoiced in spite of reviling, slander, injury, and destruction. They suffered loss of property, loss and affliction of relatives, loss of their good name. But Paul commends them, because even in their suffering, they found compassion for him and comforted him in his bonds. The Hebrews went forward, even though they were laughed at. Even when others laugh at you, Jesus is not bound by their laughter. Get out of your head and into the heart, and quit trying to figure this thing out.

I love when the boldness of the Holy Ghost comes. Then I feel like I can walk over the Empire State building. Greater is He that is in me, than he that is in the world (I John 4:4). I don't like affliction, but I love the results of affliction. I don't like having marital problems, but I love the outcome. Not long ago, somebody told my wife, "Sister Kay, I saw you making eyes at your husband." I'm glad she's making eyes at me. I say, "Honey, you make eyes all you want."

THE WORK OF SUFFERING

True godliness is usually attended by persecution. Christ died to take the curse from us, but not the cross. Piety will not shield us from suffering. The way to heaven, though full of roses in regard of the comforts of the Holy One, is full of thorns in regard to persecution. Before Israel reached Canaan, a land flowing with milk and honey, they had to go through a wilderness, with serpents and a Red Sea. So, too, the children of God in their passage to the Holy Land must meet with fiery serpents and a Red Sea of persecution.

Suffering joins Christianity and sanctity. Saints carry Christ in their hearts and the cross on their shoulders. Christ and His cross are never parted. In other words, you can't have Christ without the suffering. You can't grow in Christ and build your faith, if you never walk through the valley. Your faith does not get stronger just by sitting there.

What is the meaning of the shield of faith, the helmet of hope, and the breastplate of patience, but to imply that we must encounter suffering? (See Ephesians 6:13-17.) Christ's head was crowned with thorns, and yet we expect to be crowned with roses. If we are God's gold, it is not strange to be cast in the fire. Persecutions are pledges of God's love, badges of honor. In the sharpest trial, there is sweetest com-fort. God is fanning His wheat to make it pure. That tells me I shouldn't cast my confidence away. I may as well accept that I'm going to walk through tough times. We're going to go through things we don't understand, and we're going to have people come against us, but greater is the God in us than any tribulation that comes against us.

God wants us to know it is great to worship Him. True praise and true worship are good. It's good that I walk through the valley. It's good that I suffered and walked through that pain. I had the privilege of praying for sister Thelma Smiley, and later, when a young lady came and asked for prayer for her unsaved mother-in-law who was on life support, I was able to say with confidence, "Why, sure there's hope." If God took sister Smiley off life support, why couldn't He take this lady off it, too? In Acts 10:34, my Bible says God is no respecter of persons. If He healed me of leukemia, He can heal you of leukemia. If He healed me of a brain tumor, He can heal you of a brain tumor. If He healed you of sin, He could heal the sin in someone else's life, too. Of course, God can take her off life support. I'm confident God hears our prayers; I'm confident God is in our midst, and I'm confident that as we sing and praise Him, cancer will dry up and fall off people's lives. I believe it.

It is a good and pleasant thing to praise Him. Praising is not the grand end, but it is the grandest end we could expect. People have asked what I'd like my dying words to be. I want to say, "Lord, I love You and praise You. I thank You for a good life." It is time for believers to quit crying, "Poor, pitiful old me."

In our church family, we've had babies healed, and we've had mothers deliver babies after the doctors said they couldn't have babies. We've heard doctors say a baby in the womb wasn't right, and then rejoiced when that baby was born perfect. We've seen broken homes mended, and people saved. We've seen people healed of cancer.

I am confident in this one thing: He is able to keep that which I have committed to Him (II Timothy 1:12). I have committed my life, my salvation, my hope and my eternal security to Him. Give God what is right, instead of giving Him what is wrong. In Malachi 3:10, God said to prove Him and see if He's true. I've proved Him. We prayed He would take leukemia out of my body, and He did. We prayed He would take chemical burns out of my child, and He did. When the doctor said my child had asthma, we prayed that she wouldn't. She doesn't. We prayed for twenty-one days that our marriage wouldn't break, and praise God, He brought us closer together. We quit trying to figure it out, and started trusting in God.

Even if you're bankrupt, or in the lowest valley, you've ever been in, it is a pleasant thing to worship the

Lord and give Him praise. God has already worked it out, and already has a plan, but we're still trying to figure it out with our heads. You have to get out of the head and into the heart. God is Spirit, and the only way the heart can communicate with Him is to commune truthfully with His Spirit. His Spirit will tell the mind which way to go, what to say, and how to act and respond.

You have to be in the Spirit. You have to know God has delivered you and set you free, and that He is working things out on your behalf. When you know those things, you can begin to minister to hurting people. That's the way it is it doesn't work any other way.

THE OFFERING OF PRAISE

Genuine worship is not only good and pleasant, but it is comely. God takes sin from us when we offer it to Him. After that, what else can we offer Him but praise? He said, "I'm your God, even when they're laughing at you and persecuting you. When they say you can't make it, and the odds are against you, I'm still God, and My Word is still true." Stand on it and believe it. Get out of faith and move into the confident mode.

When I first started preaching, I wouldn't make too much noise in the pulpit because I was worried about what people might think. One day, the Lord delivered me and said, "Son, I'm the One you need to be concerned with. Quit worrying about what people think. I called you to seek and to save that which was lost. I didn't call you to make friends. Stand to your feet, preach what I put in your lips, and let Me worry about who likes it and who doesn't." Now my confidence is in God, not in what people say.

Sometimes, we just don't think. We come into a place where God is moving and sit there like He isn't even there. It is crazy, to sing our pretty little songs, and not be moved in the Spirit. That happens when we're not confident. I'm confident in who I am, and in what God wants me to do. If I just say things that soothe people's minds, I'm not doing what God called me to do. My job is to tell you to get the sin out of your life. With all the love I can muster up, my job is to walk with you through the valley. I've been through the valley, and I'm confident that if I made it, I can help you make it.

What is the supreme object of true worship? It's what God is, who He is. He is great in relation to His creatures. God uses anointed people to build schools for the mentally challenged, hospitals for the diseased, asylums for the poor. God uses His creatures to unite scattered people, and heal broken hearts. He uses them to rectify human conditions. God uses people to make a difference.

We've let our society go. One of the reasons our country is in the shape it's in is because we keep our mouths shut. We don't want to hurt anybody's feelings. God called us to tell the truth and to stand for truth. Here's the truth. If you don't love your family like Christ loved the Church, you'll lose your family. Men, if you don't treat your ladies like queens, others will. Ladies, if you don't treat your men like kings, others will. If you don't love your children the way Christ asked you to love them, when they get old enough to make a decision, you won't have to worry about them being around for you to love. We have an obligation to step out of faith into confidence. We must be confident in who we are, because there are people in our communities, people in our workplace, who are waiting for us to be confident. If we don't act like we believe what we say, why should they?

CHAPTER TWELVE

CONFIDENCE

B eing confident in who we are starts with under-standing that we are blessed. According to Matthew 5:11-12, we are blessed---even when we walk through troubled times, and it seems the devil is on our tail. It isn't because the devil has control; it is because we are blessed. We do not have to keep running from the devil; we need to start chasing him. We have that kind of power in us.

I have gone through some personal battles of my own that were nothing more than God taking me to new heights, to a new place. God is just as hungry to touch you as you are for His touch. Tell God you are tired of being who you are and are ready to be who He called you to be. I have seen God take those who seem life-less, and strengthen them and tear down old walls. I have seen folks come to church looking like a sour prune, and leave looking like a bucket of honey has been poured over them.

In Isaiah 42:8, the Bible says the glory belongs to Him. The whole earth is full of the glory of God. We look at it as though the glory comes from Heaven, but the Bible tells us the Spirit of God flows out of our being like a river of living water. That is the glory of God. The angels don't bring the glory; we bring the glory. How do you get it to come from deep within? You remember what God has done and where He brought you from, and you say, "Glory." When God's people come together and begin to give Him glory, then He comes and inhabits their praises. I want my life to be so full of glory that I can say, with Jeremiah, "It's like fire shut up in my bones." I've got some glory inside, and it has got to come out.

The Scripture says, "with His stripes we are healed" (Isaiah 53:5). You are already healed. You need to accept that healing. You say, "My home is broken." But that's only if you want it to be broken. Understand that God is already there. He already resides in you. He has called you out, and has a plan for you. Unless you curse Him, and make a mockery of Him, He will never leave you nor forsake you. When we give Him glory and praise, God shows up and things happen. People who were hurting and in bondage walk out set free, delivered, healed and restored.

THE ROCK OF OUR SALVATION

Psalms 95:1-2says,

O Come, let us sing unto the Lord: let us make a joyful noise to the rock of our salvation. Let us come before His presence with thanksgiving, and make a joyful noise unto him with psalms.

Christ is the Rock of our salvation-we are like the ship hoping for safety in the storm, the hunted fugitive flying toward a refuge, the fainting traveler throwing himself down in the shade of a rock in the desert, the steep hill with its encircling stream forming the site of a mighty fortress. Each one of these pictures tells of weakness finding comfort and aid. Each sets forth the value of the redeeming work and mighty mission of Christ our Lord. The very idea of the Rock is one of stability and strength, which cannot be removed, and upon which we may rest with security. The noble language of our creed says Christ died for us and for our salvation. He is the great example of self-sacrifice, the one who devoted Himself to death and suffering for the benefit of many.

How do we apply the benefit of Christ's work? How do we find a refuge on the Rock of salvation? By a humble and faithful realization of what He has done for us. A lot of believers say they serve Christ, but have never allowed Christ to be the solid Rock in their lives. People sometimes say, "I've heard that for fifty years." Great--- then why don't you live it? You can't live out Psalms 91:1 until something happens on the inside. At some point, you have to allow the Christ seed in your life to sprout, grow, and be watered. You have to allow that seed to produce a joyful feeling. You can face your marriage grudgingly. Your can face your job with fear. You can live with your children, hoping to the good Lord in Heaven they don't turn out the way you did. Some of us don't trust our children because we don't trust ourselves. Let Christ become the solid Rock of your salvation. When that happens, you can truly worship God.

Have you ever looked around during a service, and wondered why there are a few people just sitting there?

They want to feel what everyone else is feeling, but they can't. It may be because there are some things they are holding back from God. There is an area in my life that God is always working on. It is okay to be wrong, as long as you don't stay wrong. It's okay to have the wrong concept, as long as you get it right. It's okay to be weak, as long as you don't stay there. It becomes wrong when you don't allow Christ to be the Rock of your salvation.

God wants us to be humble, to learn to be faithful, and to realize what He has already done on our behalf. Why is it that when things go wrong, the first thing we do is go to the doctor or the counselor? That's not wrong, but why is it the **first** place we turn? We need to let Christ be the solid Rock of our lives. When things are in discord and disharmony, we should immediately get on our faces and say, "Oh God, I know Your glory is in my life, and I know You can handle this."

God can work miracles in our lives for many, many years, but when another problem comes along, we forget all about the good He's already done. We have the power to call our mind back into place. We are people of power, of great anointing, and we have great substance within us, but that substance has to be founded on Christ as the Rock of our salvation. It is Jesus Christ who saves, heals and defends us. By His Spirit, it is Jesus Christ who walks with us. That is where our confidence comes from.

When you are confident, you can boldly say to the mountain, "Get out of my way." You will never have that kind of power and strength and boldness in your life until you first allow Christ to be the Rock and Foundation of your life. A rock is solid; it can't be moved. Let the rain and the storm beat it, run it over with your equipment, but when it is all over, you still have a rock. Jesus is saying, "Yes, your are going to have tribulations and struggles, there are going to be things you don't understand, but don't let it get to you, because I am the rock of your salvation."

For every fight you have had in this life, Christ already had that fight and won. Christ conquered death, hell and the grave. He said the same power He had, you have (see John 14:12). He told us that by His stripes we are healed. If that is a reality, why do we fight sickness? Why do we fight what has already been fought?

Many of us live in fear because we have not truly made Christ the Rock of our lives. We have not honestly set our feet where they cannot be moved. Some of us need to weld our feet to the rock and say, "God, I am not moving."

MOVING FORWARD

I am tired of being pushed through life, tired of going back to the same old thing, tired of the same old battles. I am tired of praising God with a shallow understanding, and am ready to praise Him with the joy of the Lord. I am ready to make a joyful noise. If I can shout, whoop and holler until I am hoarse at a wrestling match, a ballgame, or a boxing match, then don't you think I can come into the house of the Lord and make a joyful noise? The world is seeking true believers who follow God. People are not going to follow you if you go to church saying one thing, and then go out and live another. The

Bible says, "O, clap your hands all ye people. Shout unto God with a voice of triumph" (Psalm 47:1).

It didn't say "shout with defeat," did it? If I have cancer in my body, I want people who have suffered with cancer to pray for me. I want people who have moved from faith to confidence. The world is looking for a confident church. It is nothing more than fake religion if you cannot worship with a joyful noise. When people ask about your church and your faith, joyfully, with a voice of triumph, tell them how good it is.

A banker our church had done business with some time ago stopped by one day. He remembered when our church was nothing but a barn. For over an hour, we sat in the balcony and I told him about all the miracles God was performing in this place. He said, "Now, Pastor, you know I am a Presbyterian." I told him that God is touch- ing people, no matter who they are. I told him about the little Catholic lady who came in with hearing aids, and later sold them back to her doctor. He sat there, awe- struck, as I told him about Sister Smiley and the gen- tleman who had cancer. People want to hear a voice of triumph. If we are going to be the light of the world, we have to get excited. I didn't say we all are going to have to dress alike and we sure don't all want to act alike.

Whatever I do, I am going to do it with a voice of triumph. When you need something to say, God will remind you of something He has done in your life. People can argue with theology all day long, but they cannot argue with experience. People may not be sure why we believe what we believe, but they can't deny the miracles, can't deny the excitement.

Christ is truly the Rock of our salvation and we have found Him to be true to His Word. He is strength and full of power. He is anointed and so are we; there is power in our lives. Find someone who is hurting and start telling him or her they are special and God loves them. Stop being their judge and become their friend, and see if you don't draw them in. No matter how big and bad they may seem, people want to be loved. We must go out with a voice of triumph.

PARTICULAR MINISTRIES

There are people I can never reach, but you can. God gave you your personality to reach particular people. Every person has his or her own assignment, and together, we can reach out in different areas of ministry. If Christ is truly glowing and flowing in your life, there will be a waitress who will sit down at your table and tell you all of her disappointments. There are plenty of opportunities for ministry. When you find a man of God who is anointed and taking a stand, you are responsible to join hands with him. He may not be able to go to the hospital and visit, but you can. Maybe he can't dig a ditch, but you can. That is how you build the church---everyone doing his or her part.

We should be exultant in our praise. God is God. He is supreme. He is above all. In fact, the Word says, "He is all in all" (I Corinthians 15:28). That is a reason to praise Him. The Biblical Illustrator puts it like this:

government of the world is founded upon the rea- son of things, His government of the world is founded upon the laws suited to the nature of His subjects, and His government of the world is exercised for purely benefi- cial ends. His government of the world affords oppor- tunity for rebels to be restored.

CHRIST'S LINEAGE

No matter how bad I have been, God still reaches out to me. He loves the divorcee, the sinner, and the one who is less fortunate than I. Somewhere in the lineage of Christ, there is someone who stood in and represents you. Churches have the attitude that if you don't dress right, you can't come in. Don't you know there were people who didn't dress right in the lineage of Christ? Do you think they were kicked out of the family? We must exalt Christ.

ENTHUSIASTIC PRAISE

God wants us to be enthusiastic in our praise. It is all in the way we carry ourselves. What do you think people are going to do when you enthusiastically tell them what God has done for you? True worship means I live like there is only one true God. Too often, we live like He is God when we're in trouble, but when everything is going okay, well, maybe we'll spend our money elsewhere.

We must live with the understanding that there is only one God. God is a jealous God, and He will not share His glory with the alcohol bottle, with drugs. He will not share the glory of the tithe and what it does. We give tithes so that lives just like ours can be changed. In return, we have the responsibility to be obedient. We must live like there is only one God.

Worthy worship is intelligent worship. Worship is not a meaningless act, not a burst of blind passion. It is found in the profound philosophy; it applies the grandest truth. He has already worked for you. He has already touched you. If you have honestly felt God touch you, that is reason enough to be bold, reason enough to praise His Holy Name.

Give Him all the praise due His Holy Name!

Don't Let the Rocks Cry Out!
Finding freedom in worship...

Have you ever longed for more intimacy with the Lord? For a greater understanding of His love for you? Have you found yourself standing stiff and straight in a church service, wishing there was more to worship than rigid tradition and we've-always-done-that-way praise Don't Let the Rocks Cry Out offers readers from every denomination a deeper look at the many wonderful avenues of praise and worship talked about in the Bible. In Jesus day, religious leaders wanted the disciples to stop praising Jesus. The Lord's response forms the basis for this book, if the disciples didn't praise Him, the very rocks would cry out in their place. Pastor Vining offers practical no-nonsense suggestions that shatter old stereotypes, and takes readers to a place of greater understanding and freedom in their worship of our Awesome God. With his approachable, easy-to-read style, he challenges readers to cry with him, "Ain't no rock gonna take my place!"